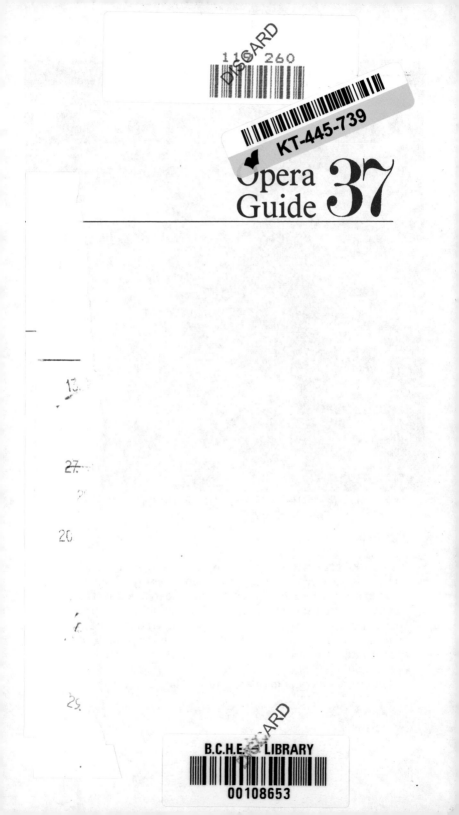

Opera
Guide **37**

Ljuba Welitsch as Salome at Covent Garden in 1949 in the production by Peter Brook, designed by Salvador Dali (photo: Donald Southern)

Preface

This series, published under the auspices of English National Opera and The Royal Opera, aims to prepare audiences to evaluate and enjoy opera in performance. Each book contains the complete text, set out in this case in transliteration, beside a modern English performing translation. The introductory essays, illustrations and musical analysis have been chosen to focus attention on some of the points of special interest in each work. We hope that, as companions to the opera should be, they are well-informed, witty and attractive.

The Royal Opera is most grateful to The Baring Foundation for sponsoring this Guide.

Nicholas John
Series Editor

37

Salome / Elektra

Richard Strauss

Opera Guide Series Editor: Nicholas John

Published in association with
English National Opera and The Royal Opera
and assisted by a generous donation from the Baring Foundation

John Calder · London
Riverrun Press · New York

First published in Great Britain, 1988 by
John Calder (Publishers) Ltd.,
18 Brewer Street, London W1R 4AS

First published in the U.S.A., 1988 by
Riverrun Press Inc.,
1170 Broadway, New York, NY 10001

BRITISH LIBRARY CATALOGUING IN PUBLICATION DATA

Strauss, Richard, *1864-1949*
    Salome and Elektra.—(Opera guide, 37).
    1. Opera in German. Strauss, Richard, 1864-
    1949. Elektra & Salome. Critical studies
    I. Title   II. Hofmannsthal, Hugo von, *1874-*
    1929   III. Wilde, Oscar, *1854-1900*
    IV. Strauss, Richard, *1864-1949* Elektra
    V. Series
    782.1'2

    ISBN 0-7145-4131-1

LIBRARY OF CONGRESS CATALOGING IN PUBLICATION DATA

Strauss, Richard, 1864-1949.
    [Salome. Libretto. English & German]
    Salome; &, Elektra / Richard Strauss.
        p.   cm. — — (Opera guide; 37)
    Includes librettos in German after Oscar Wilde's tragedy (Salome)
and by Hugo von Hofmannsthal based on Sophocles (Elektra) with
English translations.
    "Published in association with English National Opera and The
Royal Opera."
    Discography: p. 142
    Bibliography: p. 143
    ISBN 0-7145-4131-1 (pbk.) : $7.95
    1. Strauss, Richard, 1864-1949. Salome. 2. Strauss, Richard,
1864-1949. Elektra. 3. Operas—Librettos. I. Wilde, Oscar.
1854-1900 Salome. II. Strauss, Richard, 1864-1949. Elektra.
Libretto. 1988. III. English National Opera. IV. Royal Opera
House (London, England) V. Title. VI. Title: Salome. VII. Title:
Elektra. VIII. Series.
ML50.S918S32 1988 (Case)

782.1'2—dc19

88-6444
CIP
MN

Typeset in Plantin by Maggie Spooner Typesetting, London.

Printed by Camelot Press Ltd., Southampton.

Contents

List of Illustrations

Richard Strauss and the unveiling of 'Salomé'

Paul Banks

In November 1895, while he was serving a two-year prison sentence for acts of gross indecency, Oscar Wilde was declared bankrupt and, following his death almost exactly five years later in Paris, his English creditors received a mere three shillings in the pound. An official of the Court of Bankruptcy took the view that Wilde's literary works were 'of no value, and could never command any interest whatsoever', and it seems that because of public disapprobation Wilde would probably not have dissented from this view. Both men failed to anticipate the growth of Wilde's European reputation: by December 1905 his estate was solvent, largely due to the royalties from German translations and productions of his works, a wry irony in view of Wilde's antipathy to German culture. It was not the social comedies, however, which had established themselves on the English stage before Wilde's trials, that initially captured attention, but a symbolic tragedy in French whose public performance had been banned in England by the Lord Chamberlain: *Salomé*. During the author's lifetime it had a solitary production in Paris (1896); but in German translation it appeared first at Breslau (1901), and then in a triumphantly successful staging by Max Reinhardt at the Kleines Theater in Berlin, where it ran for over 200 performances.

To be understood, this unexpected Berlin success needs to be seen in a wider context: it was one of a series of premières there which in 1902-3 captured attention. One common feature of the plays concerned — Strindberg's *Rausch*, Wedekind's *Erdgeist*, Gorky's *Nachtasyl* and Hofmannsthal's *Elektra* as well as Wilde's *Salomé* — was their portrayal of demonic feminine sexuality, a motif which also invaded the visual arts at about the same time (e.g. Franz von Stuck: *The Kiss of the Sphinx* (c. 1895); Ferdinand Khnopf: *The Caresses of the Sphinx* (1896); Edvard Munch: *Vampire* (1896-1902), *Madonna* (1895-1902)). According to one of the most fervent admirers of Wilde's *Salomé*, the Viennese satirist and cultural commentator Karl Kraus, Reinhardt's production of the play ignored the symbolic content, replacing it with an extreme realism. Significantly, it was this production which Richard Strauss attended while working on an operatic adaptation of Wilde's play and Reinhardt's lack of interest in the text's symbolism is paralleled in (and may have influenced) the opera. Strauss's draft was completed in September 1904, and the full score finished on June 20, 1905.

Although Reinhardt's Berlin production (including the acting of Gertrud Eysoldt as Salome) may well have contributed to Strauss's treatment of the play, it was appropriately Viennese culture which provided him with the initial stimulus, for Wilde's works and aesthetic views had a notable conceptual and creative impact in the Austrian capital. Both Kraus and Hugo von Hofmannsthal responded to Wilde's ideas about the role of masks in life and literature, and Viennese composers such as Schreker (*Der Geburtstag der Infantin* (1908); *Die Gezeichneten* (1913-15)) and Zemlinsky (*Eine florentinische Tragödie* (1916); *Der Zwerg* (1921)) were later to follow Strauss's example in using Wildean texts as the basis for stage works. It was a boyhood friend of Kraus, Anton Lindner, who in 1901 or 1902 offered to provide Strauss with a libretto based on Wilde's play and whetted the composer's appetite with an

7

passages
wavy work.

ingenious re-writing of the opening scene. But it was some time before Strauss realised that with judicious cutting — to 'purge the piece of purple passages' — Wilde's original text (translated by Hedwig Lachmann) would become 'quite a good libretto'.

Strauss's retrospective assessment of the quality of the text of his opera (made in 1942), seems unduly cautious. The French writer Romain Rolland — an admirer of Strauss, who was not uncritical of some aspects of *Salome* — in 1905 offered the composer a more apt evaluation of the structural qualities of the text:

> . . . the libretto, as you have arranged it, is admirably suited to the stage; it is at the same time picturesque, and compact, concentrated: it is a dramatic crescendo from beginning to end.
>
> Richard Strauss, Romain Rolland, *Correspondence*, ed. R. Myers (London, 1968)

NB.

Indeed, in terms of compression and opportunities for the portrayal, juxtaposition and interaction of characters within a clear dramatic framework, the text of *Salome* was probably not bettered by any of the libretti the composer subsequently set. Perhaps in his old age Strauss came to agree with Rolland's ethical doubts about the opera's 'repugnant and unwholesome' subject matter. Similar objections had been raised by Gustav Mahler when he heard of Strauss's intention to set Wilde's text but Mahler's fears were silenced when he heard the music in May 1905. Both he and Strauss were in Strasbourg to conduct concerts at the Alsatian Musical Festival, and Strauss insisted on taking Mahler and his wife, Alma, to a piano shop, so that he could play them his recently composed opera. Alma reported many years later that:

> Strauss played and sang incomparably well. Mahler was overwhelmed. We came to the dance — it was missing. 'Haven't got it done yet,' Strauss said and played on to the end, leaving this yawning gap. 'Isn't it rather risky,' Mahler remarked, 'simply leaving out the dance, and then writing it in later when you're not in the same mood?' Strauss laughed his light-hearted laugh: 'I'll fix that all right.'
>
> Alma Mahler, *Gustav Mahler, Memories and Letters*, ed. D. Mitchell (London, 1973)

Mahler immediately began to plan for an early production of the opera at the Vienna Court Opera, but despite all his powers of persuasion as Director, he was unable to induce the censorship office of the Court Theatres to allow the work to be performed. As in London, one of the main stumbling blocks seems to have been the stage representation of biblical characters, and no doubt the author's reputation did much to strengthen opposition to the work. While the sensationally successful world première was eventually given at the Dresden Court Opera under Ernst von Schuch on December 9, 1905, it was not until 1918, after the collapse of the Habsburg monarchy, that the work was finally performed at what had been the Vienna Court Opera.

The ban on *Salome* in Vienna extended only as far as the Court Theatres and in 1907 the work was given at the Volkstheater in a touring production from Breslau. This inspired the painter Gustav Klimt to return to a related biblical subject which he had provocatively explored for the first time in 1901: Judith and Holofernes. In both paintings Klimt replaces the conventional iconographical representation of Judith as a pious avenging widow (e.g. in Cristofano Allori (1577-1621), *Judith*) with an image of a sexually provocative

*Geneviève Vix
as Salome
(Royal Opera
House Archives)*

femme fatale in a state of erotic excitement clutching the decapitated head of the Assyrian general. Thus transformed, the subject bears a close relationship to Salome as portrayed by Wilde and Strauss, and both paintings were and are still often misnamed 'Salome'. Yet even in the earlier version the relationship between pictorial representation and decorative elements is strikingly different from that in the Salomé paintings by Gustave Moreau which either directly, or through the literary celebrations of them by J.-K. Huysmans, formed one of the influences absorbed by Wilde. For Moreau the glittering jewel-like flecks of paint form a decorative veil over the illusion of three-dimensional forms without interfering with their representational integrity. In *Judith I*, however, Klimt is already employing flat, two-dimensional

9

patterns that contrast strongly with the sense of roundness reserved for the half-nude female figure, and that actually separate the head from the torso. This stylised decapitation is a visual motif whose origins lie in the high-necked collar of a plaster sculpture entitled (significantly) *Mask*, by the Belgian symbolist painter Ferdinand Khnopf. In 1898 a photograph of the bust was included in *Ver Sacrum*, the journal of the Vienna Secession and Klimt employed this image in a number of female portraits (e.g. *Emile Flöge* (1902), *Fritza Riedler* (1906) and *Adele Bloch-Bauer I* (1907) as well as *Judith II* (1909)). Particularly in *Judith I* it combines with the abrupt interaction of painting and frame to reinforce the violence of the subject in a way which contrasts strongly with the static passivity of Moreau's images.

Originally Wilde planned a Klimt-like duplication of the central act of violence by making Salomé both the instigator and the victim of a decapitation, though eventually such neat patterning was abandoned in favour of characterisation and symbolism. Three of the characters — Narraboth, Salomé and Herod — are obsessive voyeurs, and all are warned of the dangers of their obsession. But Herod also refuses to look at what he fears: he has Jochanaan hidden in a cistern and Narraboth's corpse removed from sight. So, when he learns to fear Salomé, he has her obliterated beneath the shields — an unmistakable visual metaphor for psychological repression. The power and violence of this image suggest that what is being repressed is more than just the memory of a sexually depraved step-daughter: the psycho-analytical association of decapitation with fears of castration offers a revealing insight, since Herodias has already taunted Herod with accusations of impotence. Moreover, as Edward Lucie-Smith has shown, the iconography of the Salomé story includes occasional homosexual references, as in F.U. Bachiacca's *The Beheading of John the Baptist* (1539?), and Wilde makes it clear that both the Page and Herod are erotically attracted to Narraboth. More importantly Salomé's offer to give Narraboth 'a little green flower' is a barely concealed indication that her ostensible heterosexuality must be understood as a substitution for homoerotic relationships and that at this level the work takes on autobiographical connotations: green carnations were a badge of Parisian homosexuals which Wilde adopted in the 1890s. This hint of an underlying autobiographical content is given graphic confirmation by an astonishing photograph of Wilde dressed as *Salomé*. Like Wilde, Salomé achieves spiritual/artistic insight after tasting the fruits of her socially unacceptable erotic desires.

Neither Klimt nor Strauss show any inclination to explore the homoerotic potential of their material, but both confront the threatening, terrifying figure of *la belle dame sans merci* and, in seeking appropriately vivid means of portrayal, are led to extend their technical resources as artists. In the years following *Judith I* the decorative symbolism of Klimt's female portraits became more explicit and occupied an increasingly substantial proportion of each canvas. He reached an extreme point in *Adele Bloch-Bauer I*, with its Egyptian eye-triangles and stylised peacock feathers — presumably un-intentional parallels to the voyeurism of Wilde's play and the peacocks Herod offers Salomé in a vain effort to escape the consequences of his ill-considered oath. In *Judith II* the figurative element is much reduced in comparison with its predecessor, and warm flesh tones are almost entirely absent; the generally darker but more varied palette, which generates striking contrasts, sharp contours and the claw-like hands all contribute to a far more intimidating treatment of the subject. In a similar way Strauss extended techniques he had

Oscar Wilde in costume as Salome (photo: Collection Viollet)

tried out tentatively in the earlier symphonic poems, and created a musical idiom capable of an exceptionally vivid portrayal of terror, anger and violence. This first emerges as Salome attempts to seduce Jokanaan. He rejects her opening stanza celebrating the whiteness of his body, stinging the young woman into a violent repudiation of the initial object of her obsession at the beginning of her second stanza ('Your flesh is horrible.'). Although Salome has earlier been characterised by music that is tonally, thematically and rhythmically restless, this is the first point in the score that such qualities, heightened by disturbingly heterogeneous orchestration, dissonant harmony and more angular vocal lines, take on a threatening quality. Similar passages occur with increasing frequency as the drama progresses, associated not only with Salome, but also Herod's growing fear of her. More vehement scoring (including, at times, some virtuoso whole-tone scale passages for the timpani and the separation of the orchestra into sharply contrasted stratas of instrumental colour) and dissonant, non-functional harmony give the music a nightmarish intensity comparable both expressively and technically with the expressionism of Schoenberg's Five Orchestral Pieces Op. 16 (1909). At such

11

Hans Hotter as Jokanaan in 1952 (photo: Metropolitan Opera Archives)

moments Strauss goes beyond the limits of functional tonality, relying on various devices, including ostinati and pedal points, to assert pitch centres within a maelstrom of orchestral sound.

The expressive directness of Strauss's music embodies an aesthetic strategy somewhat different from that encapsulated in Wilde's deliberately artificial text. Writing about the ideal drama, Wilde wrote that dramatic art gave its characters:

> a language different from that of actual use, a language full of resonant music and sweet rhythm, made stately by solemn cadence, or made delicate by fanciful rhyme, jewelled with wonderful words, and enriched with lofty diction. She clothed her children in strange raiment and gave them masks . . . 'The Decay of Living', *De Profundis and Other Writings*, (Harmondsworth, 1986).

This is an apt description of the linguistic quality of *Salomé* where the 'strange raiment' is an alien language; a similar effect is present to a lesser extent in the incomplete *Florentine Tragedy* where a deliberately archaic blank verse idiom is adopted. It seems that Puccini, who seriously considered the latter fragment as the basis of an opera in 1906 and again in 1912, was interested in the historical setting of the story but he would probably have been no more concerned to find a musical equivalent of Wilde's stylised syntax and vocabulary than was Zemlinsky in his setting. The mere translation into German or Italian to some extent compromised the artificiality of Wilde's language, and, in the case of *Salomé*, the phonetic qualities of Lachmann's version are inevitably more hard-edged than those of the French original. In 1905 Strauss, hoping for an early production in Paris, attempted to marry his music with Wilde's original text and sought advice from Romain Rolland. The resulting correspondence, particularly Rolland's contribution, offers fascinating insights into the contrasting musical implications of French and German, not least the differing intonation patterns:

> You don't like Debussy's musical declamation, my friend? . . . As refined, aristocratic society French declamation it is perfect . . . it has opened up the way to true French musical declamation. If you do not like this kind of recitative with its very efficient lines, bear in mind that Wagnerian declamation seems barbarous to us . . . when it is applied to our language. A French middle-class man, or even a working class man, never uses those vocal leaps which one finds all the time in *The Mastersingers*.

The deliberate barbarity in Strauss's opera can in part be traced back to an exaggeration of post-Wagnerian German musical declamation.

Wilde's handling of language, though owing much to Flaubert, Mallarmé and most of all, Maeterlinck, also reveals parallels with Moreau and anticipations of Klimt's handling of a similar subject. The vocabulary of *Salomé* offers a colourful aural surface: in both Moreau and Wilde jewels have not merely a symbolic or dramatic function; they also offer an excuse for virtuoso displays of colouristic effects. But in Wilde's text, as in Klimt's *Judith II*, the recurring decorative elements are often more substantial — not just words but phrases — establishing patterns which counterpoint the narrative thrust in the former and the representational component in the latter. In the play recurring phrases and images — e.g. 'Comme la princesse Salomé est belle ce soir!', 'Vous la regardez toujours', 'Il peut arriver un malheur' — lose on repetition something of their effect as characterisation or evocation, and take on instead an hypnotic, ritualistic quality, weaving patterns of cross-reference through the text. For Rolland such verbal repetitions were inconsequential and even laughable — 'literary jargon' — but for Wilde they were an important aspect of the play's pervasive musicality, 'refrains whose recurring motifs make *Salomé* so like a piece of music and bind it together as a ballad'.

Wilde was not particularly interested in music, and many of his frequent assertions about the musicality of language may well have had their origins in Walter Pater's well-known dictum that 'all art tends towards the condition of music'. But in the case of *Salomé*, Wilde's reference to 'recurring motifs' suggests another influence: Wagner. During the 1880s and 1890s the impact of Wagner's ideas within artistic circles on both sides of the Channel was pervasive and when, in 1891, Wilde made contact with members of the circle around Stephan Mallarmé in Paris, he gained access to the centre of Wagner's literary influence in France. The technique of using verbal leitmotifs found in so much post-symbolist writing had its origins in the work of members of this group. Of course Strauss's music for the operatic stage was also founded on a post-Wagnerian use of leitmotifs, but it is at this point of apparent convergence between linguistic and musical technique in *Salome* that the aesthetic divergence between dramatist and composer is most starkly revealed. Wilde adapted a musico-dramatic device as a means of undermining the status of dramatic characterisation by superimposing a decorative linguistic veil; Strauss deployed the same technique as one component in his breathtakingly vivid characterisations of the central figures in the drama.

It seems unlikely that Wilde would have commended Strauss's dramatic strategy, since he had criticised Shakespeare for the 'over-importance assigned to characterisation' in his plays. For his part Strauss virtually ignores Wilde's more decorative verbal repetitions. Many were removed when the text of the play was compressed and few such phrases are associated with particular musical ideas in the opera. Moreover Strauss is generally not concerned to respond to recurring images — the moon, which, as Karl Kraus pointed out, plays such a crucial role in the text and the visual symbolism of the play, has no musical embodiment, and most of the stage instructions referring to its changing aspects are omitted from the score. One recurrent feature which does capture Strauss's attention is the beating wings of the angel of death first heard by Jokanaan ('Leave me, I say! For there in that palace I hear the rustling wings of death's dark angel . . .'), and twice later by Herod (both passages begin 'It's so cold here.'), but the result is an unwelcome intrusion of naive musical realism (rushing semi-quaver chromatic scales in strings and woodwind). Ravel, who otherwise admired 'the formidable unity of the work', was surely right to regret such non-thematic literalism in a score otherwise remarkable for the sophistication and variety of its thematic processes.

The disjunction between dramatist and composer is nowhere clearer than in Salome's Dance. For Wilde art was a veil, and he spoke of wanting 'scented clouds', that would rise from braziers of perfume and veil the stage of *Salomé* from time to time: inevitably the Dance of the Seven Veils had a special, mysterious significance for him. In the presentation copy of the first edition he gave to Aubrey Beardsley (now in the Sterling Library, University of London) Wilde wrote: 'For the only artist who, beside myself, knows what the dance of the seven veils is, and can see that invisible dance.' Strauss has no interest in an invisible dance: within his reading of the text this is the moment when the voyeuristic desires of both Herod and the audience are finally satisfied as the sensual is made visible. A price has to be paid by all later: a confrontation with images so terrible that they have to be repressed. The music prefigures this outcome, moving from teasing seductiveness to a balletic agressiveness unmatched until Stravinsky's *Rite of Spring*. Wilde's Salomé may offer Herod a fleeting insight into existential mysteries; Strauss reveals the awesome fusion of sexual desire and anger which motivates her.

The Dance is in some ways a problematic passage in the opera. Mahler's doubts about Strauss's ability to completely re-enter the mood of the work were perhaps justified: it is certainly noticeable that the opening of the Dance is the one point in the opera where an oriental style is attempted. Elsewhere the music may be exotic and luxurious, yet it resolutely avoids such pseudo-orientalism. Nevertheless as an element in the characterisation of Salome the Dance is consistent and significant, and any aesthetic problems it raises are not the result of its divergence from Wilde's conception of the episode. On the other hand, in the following passage the strategy of poet and composer fruitfully converge. Here Wilde's refrain-like repetitions of Salomé's demand for the head of Jokanaan are more than merely decorative quasi-musical figures, and constitute a dramatic effect of immense power. This is one point where Strauss responds to Wilde's verbal repetitions, although even here he does not treat the seven demands for the Baptist's head as a simple musical refrain, but as a series of transformations of two related but distinct melodic ideas. The first demand is made laughingly:

The second is accompanied by the leitmotif associated most consistently with Salome's revenge [14b]:

15

The third and fourth demands are based on transformations of [14b], while the fifth fuses elements from the vocal line of Ex. 2 with that of Ex. 1:

The sixth returns to [14b]. In the last Salome aggressively refuses not only Herod's offer of the 'veil of the sanctuary', but also the tonal implications of the accompanying trills. Her major/minor transformation of Ex. 1 ignores the D (major) asserted by the lower pitches, and adopts the E♭/B♭ of the upper notes:

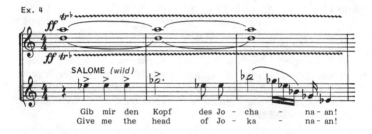

Herod admits defeat, accepting both Salome's will and one of her themes:

Here leitmotif technique is employed merely for emphasis on an aspect of the relationship between Herod and Salome which is articulated in the text. Earlier Strauss uses the same device to make explicit an aspect of their relationship which is only tacitly indicated by Wilde: when Herodias accuses Herod of being afraid of Jokanaan he replies 'Ich habe vor niemandem Angst' (the English version of the play, attributed to Lord Alfred Douglas and revised by Wilde himself, gives this as 'I am afraid of no man'), accompanied by the first four notes of [5], one of the motifs associated primarily with Salome's childlike innocence. Similarly during Salome's attempted seduction of Jokanaan she repeats 'Ich will deinen Mund küssen' ('I long for your mouth's kisses'), always to [12]. The prophet urges her to seek forgiveness for her sins from Christ ('Go, seek Him'), to music of radiant diatonic simplicity [13], but the graceful incorporation of [12] into the accompaniment makes Salome's inattention evident. Again the verbal refrain is far from being merely decorative: it is an essential element in the portrayal of Salome's growing obsession, and Strauss reflects this on two musical levels. The obvious thematic reinforcement of the verbal refrain is given particular force by the theme's prominent use of a minor third, an interval which pervades the

Maria Ewing at Covent Garden (photo: Zoë Dominic)

melodic contours of the opera like a motivic obsession (e.g. [4c], [14b], and the minor mode transformation of [11]).

At the end of Salome's pathological *Liebestod* both the theme and the text undergo expressive transformations. Salome's necrophiliac kiss has a bitter taste and she thinks this may be the taste of love: the orchestra responds with a transformation of [12] which expands the opening minor third to a fourth and gives the theme clear (though as yet unfulfilled) cadential implications:

Ex. 6

'They tell me that the taste of love is bitter': the orchestra repeats the transformation in dissonant counterpoint before Salome herself triumphantly sings it for the one and only time, 'I have kissed your mouth'. Having fulfilled her obsessive desire Salome is released from it, and the theme's inhibited cadential power is unleashed by the long-awaited closure in C# major.

The aptness of [12] is relatively esoteric, resulting from the thematic and intervallic processes of the opera as a whole. More typically the vividness of Strauss's musical characterisation is founded on the ability to invent highly distinctive themes which seem to assert the appropriateness of their association with a particular character, event, mood or idea. Trying to pin down the nature of this appropriateness with adjectives tends to circumscribe rather than expand understanding of the relationship: Strauss's art is founded on the notion that themes [5], [4b] and [22] are in some obvious yet multi-faceted way appropriate to an impetuous young girl, a God-obsessed prophet and a nagging wife. A more daring procedure is sometimes used: in order to offer a commentary on a situation Strauss employs a theme which appears to be inappropriate to its ostensible context. The first appearance of Jokanaan offers a fascinating example. He has already been heard prophesying from the subterranean cistern and a number of themes, including [4a], have been associated with him but, while he is brought for Salome to see, a new idea begins to emerge from the depths of the orchestra. At his appearance on stage the slow-moving, wide-stepping, diatonic outlining of the tonic chord of the opening of [8] is consistent with the musical characterisation of the prophet which Strauss has already established (though the occasional dissonances are less typical), but the continuation is unexpected. The D# is functionally ambiguous: it may be heard enharmonically as an Eb, implying a juxtaposition of C minor and C major, or it may be a chromatic appoggiatura challenging the fundamental diatonicism of the passage. It is the latter interpretation which is subsequently exploited: the melody continues to move in semi-tones accompanied by side-slipping seventh chords which cadence on B major: the convoluted melodic line, the chromaticism, the tonal instability and the dissonances all sound inappropriate to a musical embodiment of Jokanaan.

A clue to this passage's significance is provided by Strauss's modification of

18

the stage direction that follows Jokanaan's appearance. Where Lachmann's translation corresponds to Wilde's English version ('Salomé looks at him and steps slowly back') Strauss strengthens the first clause — 'Salome, absorbed in his appearance . . .'. Theme [8] may thus be intended to refer not to Jokanaan (as is sometimes assumed) but to Salome's perception of him. There is further confirmation of this association when Salome describes his body ('How pale and wan he looks! As though he were carved out of ivory.'). The theme is stated by the oboes in octaves and Salome's doubling of the line does not begin until the third note (emphasising, perhaps, that she is not interested in him as a prophet); thereafter the tortuous continuation offers an apt accompaniment to the mixture of repulsion and attraction she experiences. The link between

Grace Bumbry as Salome at Covent Garden (photo: Anthony Crickmay)

the theme and Salome is made even clearer by the tonal content of these two statements: the first begins in C major, a key already associated with Jokanaan (and more generally the world around Salome), and cadences in B major, the key which will emerge for the first time (and with notable cadential power) at the beginning of the first stanza of Salome's attempted seduction of Jokanaan ('Your body wakens my desire, Jokanaan!'). When Salome sings [8] it cadences on C# major, the key which throughout the opera tends to be associated with her.

Juxtapositions of keys are not the only harmonic means Strauss employs to differentiate characters. In *Salome*, functional tonality ranges in character from the diatonicism of some of Jokanaan's music, to the extended tonality often associated with Herod. But the varieties of functional tonality form only part of a broader spectrum of harmonic types which includes bitonality and neo-tonal music. In the latter conventional harmonic structure is often abandoned, the music is dissonant, and chord progressions no longer function as a means of establishing the primacy of one tonic chord; instead other devices (e.g. pedal points and ostinati) are used to assert the primacy of a single note. So in his search for ever more potent forms of musical contrast, Strauss can juxtapose different types of harmony, a device used most starkly at the end of the opera. Much of Salome's closing scene, like her music elsewhere in the score, uses a restless form of extended tonality but, within this context, C# minor, and later C# major, are repeatedly affirmed with increasingly direct functional harmonic progressions. Pitched against this are Herod's two interruptions, the second of which brings the work to its brutal conclusion. Both are highly dissonant passages on the brink of atonality which assert C as their pitch centre. Thus the dramatic confrontation is underpinned by the conflict between C# and C, and also by the opposition of extended tonality and neo-tonality.

The music of *Salome* is not just concerned, however, with characterisation and interaction of the *dramatis personae*, but the evocation of the changing emotional landscapes against which the drama is acted out. This is not a task the dramatist has to embrace: dramatic dialogue can merely embody or imply states of mind, moods which it does not have to describe. Such elusiveness appealed to Wilde, and it absolved him from the daunting task of finding words in the final scene to describe the emotional state of a young woman who has just kissed the lips of a decapitated head: Salomé's fragmentary final utterances do not offer an exploration of her psyche, but leave the audience to reconstruct the unspeakable. The composer cannot allow himself quite such reticence: he has to create at least an aural backcloth appropriate to Salome's inarticulateness. Strauss's imaginative response is extraordinary:

Ex. 6

Conventional triadic harmony is abandoned: a semitone trill and a piercing fragment of melody in the high woodwind are suspended above a low, dissonant sonority in the strings and brass. All three elements appear elsewhere in the opera. The trills and woodwind melody [11] are associated with Salome's obsession with Jokanaan, and the prototype of the dissonant sonority emerges initially as Salome looks into the depths of the cistern for the first time. There the lowest note was a C; at the end, as she contemplates her own inner darkness it is a C#. Yet the resonances of this passage are more complex and far-reaching than the sum of earlier associations. It is striking that it is not the kiss itself which offers Salome erotic satisfaction (indeed Ex. 7 suggests it is an empty experience), but the subsequent realisation that her wish has been fulfilled. The transition from the non-tonal dissonance of Ex. 7 to a final, long delayed tonal cadence in C# major (prepared for but then postponed at the end of Salome's previous solo) mirrors this journey from non-experience to quasi-fulfilment.

In January 1907 Mahler heard two performances of *Salome* in Berlin and in a letter to Alma he touched on an aesthetic issue which, contrary to his hope, time has done nothing to resolve:

> The impression it made was stronger than ever and I am firmly convinced that it is one of the greatest masterpieces of our time. I cannot make out the drift of it, and can only surmise that it is the voice of the 'earth-spirit' speaking from the heart of genius, a spirit which does not indeed make a dwelling-place for itself to suit human taste but in accordance with its own unfathomable needs. Perhaps in time I shall gain a clearer understanding of this 'cocoon' it has spun for itself.

Romain Rolland, who also admired the music but disliked the subject matter even more emphatically, argued that Strauss at least tried to feel pity for his 'unfortunate heroine', and Wilde, who in the years following his release from prison planned (but never wrote) an essay 'which would have allowed pity into his aesthetic system', might well have appreciated this aspect of the score. The closing pages of the opera embody a qualified compassion which coexists with, but cannot be reconciled with, a sense of horror. Strauss's challenging refusal to resolve the tensions between these two responses to the drama both sustains and mirrors the fractured aesthetic response to the opera characterised by Mahler and Rolland. The process of adapting Wilde's play as an opera in the post-Wagnerian German tradition, coupled with Strauss's own penchant for vivid characterisation, contributed both to an unveiling of Wilde's Salomé and also, in part, to a repainting of her portrait with a different palette. Miraculously what emerges is not an operatic trivialisation or simplification, but a complex portrayal which continues to be richly provocative.

Sources include the biographies of Wilde by H. Montgomery Hyde and R. Ellmann (London, 1976 and 1987), *Karl Kraus, Apocalyptic Satirist* by E. Timms (London, 1987), *Gustav Klimt* by A. Comini (London, 1975), *Eroticism in Western Art* by E. Lucie-Smith (London, 1972) and *The Operas of Puccini* by W. Ashbrook (London, 1969).

Thematic Guide

Many of the themes from *Salome* have been identified in the articles by numbers in square brackets, which refer to the themes set out in these pages. The themes are also identified by the numbers in square brackets at the corresponding points in the libretto, so that the words can be related to the musical themes.

Herod's infatuation

[7]

[8]
Breit

[9]

[10]

[11]

[12]

[13]

[14a]

[14b]

[15]

[16]

[17]

[18]

[19]

[20]

[21]

[22]
hässlich
kreischend

24

Salome

Music Drama in One Act

by Richard Strauss

after Oscar Wilde's tragedy
in the German translation of Hedwig Lachmann

English translation by Tom Hammond

Salome was first performed in Dresden on December 9, 1905. The first
performance in England was at Covent Garden on December 8, 1910.
The first performance in the United States was at the Metropolitan
Opera House, New York on January 22, 1907.

*Josephine Barstow performs Salome's Dance of the Seven Veils at ENO in the production by Joachim
Herz, designed by Rudolf Heinrich, 1981 (photo: Donald Southern)*

CHARACTERS

Herod Antipas *Tetrarch of Judea*	*tenor*
Herodias *wife of the Tetrarch*	*mezzo-soprano*
Salome *daughter of Herodias*	*soprano*
Jokanaan *the Prophet*	*baritone*
Narraboth *a young Syrian*	*tenor*
A Page of Herodias	*mezzo-soprano*
Five Jews	*4 tenors, 1 bass*
Two Nazarenes	*tenor, bass*
Two Soldiers	*basses*
A Cappadocian	*bass*
A Slave	

A great terrace in the Palace of Herod.

'Salome' in Amsterdam, 1988, produced by Harry Kupfer, designed by Wilfried Werz (photo: Jaap Pieper)

Scene One.

NARRABOTH

[1]
[2]

How fair the royal Princess Salome
looks tonight.

Wie schön ist die Prinzessin Salome
heute Nacht!

PAGE

See, the moon has risen, she looks
strangely eerie, she's like a woman who
rises from her grave.

Sieh' die Mondscheibe, wie sie seltsam
aussieht. Wie eine Frau, die aufsteigt aus
dem Grab.

NARRABOTH

She's strangely lovely, like some
diminutive princess whose feet are little
snow white doves. She might be dancing [1]
up there.

Sie ist sehr seltsam. Wie eine kleine
Prinzessin, deren Füsse weisse Tauben
sind. Man könnte meinen, sie tanzt.

PAGE

She's like a lifeless woman, still gliding
slowly aloft.

Wie eine Frau, die tot ist. Sie gleitet
langsam dahin.

Noise in the banqueting hall.
[3]

FIRST SOLDIER

What a commotion! Who's that howling
now, like jackals in the desert?

Was für ein Aufruhr! Was sind das für
wilde Tiere, die da heulen?

SECOND SOLDIER

Those Jews, there.

Die Juden.

(dryly)

Oh, they never change. They quarrel
about religion all the time.

Sie sind immer so. Sie streiten über ihre
Religion.

FIRST SOLDIER

I find it ridiculous, getting heated over
such matters.

Ich finde es lächerlich, über solche
Dinge zu streiten.

NARRABOTH
(warmly)

How fair the royal Princess Salome
looks this evening!

Wie schön ist die Prinzessin Salome
heute Abend!

PAGE
(anxiously)

You stare too much at her. Your eyes
never leave her! It's always dang'rous
looking at people here, just like that.
Terrible things may happen.

Du siehst sie immer an. Du siehst sie zu
viel an. Es ist gefährlich, Menschen auf
diese Art anzusehn. Schreckliches kann
geschehn.

NARRABOTH

She is so fair here this evening.

[1] Sie ist sehr schön heute Abend.

FIRST SOLDIER

See how grim the Tetrarch looks.

Der Tetrarch sieht finster drein.

SECOND SOLDIER

Yes, how he looks.

Ja, er sieht finster drein.

FIRST SOLDIER

But who's he staring at?

Auf wen blickt er?

SECOND SOLDIER

I don't know.

Ich weiss nicht.

NARRABOTH

How pale is her lovely face. I've never seen her look quite so pale before. She's like the reflection of a milk-white rosebud, caught in a mirror of silver.

[1] Wie blass die Prinzessin ist. Niemals habe ich sie so blass gesehn. Sie ist wie der Schatten einer weissen Rose in einem silbernen Spiegel.

PAGE
(very anxiously)

You must not keep looking. You stare at her far too much. Terrible things may happen.

Du musst sie nicht ansehn. Du siehst sie zu viel an. Schreckliches kann geschehn.

THE VOICE OF JOKANAAN
(from the cistern)

After me shall come another, one far mightier than I. I am not worthy to unfasten the latchet upon his shoes. When he comes then shall all the desolate places be joyful. When he comes then shall the eyes of the blind man see day again. When he comes the ears of the deaf shall be opened.

Nach mir wird Einer kommen, der ist [4] stärker als ich. Ich bin nicht wert, ihm zu lösen den Riemen an seinen Schuhn. [4c] Wenn er kommt, werden die verödeten Stätten frohlocken. Wenn er kommt, werden die Augen der Blinden den Tag sehn. Wenn er kommt, die Ohren der Tauben geöffnet.

SECOND SOLDIER

Make him silent!

[4c] Heiss ihn schweigen!

FIRST SOLDIER

But he's a holy man.

[4b] Er ist ein heil'ger Mann.

SECOND SOLDIER

He's forever shouting all that nonsense.

[4c] Er sagt immer lächerliche Dinge.

FIRST SOLDIER

And he's so kind . . .When I bring him his food he always thanks me, every time.

[4b] Er ist sehr sanft. Jeden Tag, den ich ihm zu essen gebe, dankt er mir.

A CAPPADOCIAN

Who is he?

[4c] Wer ist es?

FIRST SOLDIER

He's a prophet.

Ein Prophet.

CAPPADOCIAN

What do they call him?

Wie ist sein Name?

FIRST SOLDIER

Jokanaan.

Jochanaan.

CAPPADOCIAN

Where does he come from?

Woher kommt er?

FIRST SOLDIER

From the desert. Crowds of his disciples always flocked to his side.

[4b] Aus der Wüste. Eine Schar von Jüngern war dort immer um ihn.

CAPPADOCIAN

What does he talk about?

[4c] Wovon redet er?

FIRST SOLDIER

There's no-one here understands what he says.

[4b] Unmöglich ist's, zu verstehn, was er sagt.

CAPPADOCIAN

Then may I see him? [4c] Kann man ihn sehn?

FIRST SOLDIER

No, that's forbidden by the Tetrarch. Nein, der Tetrarch hat es verboten.

NARRABOTH
(*highly excited*)

See, the Princess is rising. She has left [1] Die Prinzessin erhebt sich! Sie verlässt
the table. She seems most upset. She's [2] die Tafel. Sie ist sehr erregt. Sie kommt
coming out. hierher.

PAGE

Don't stare at her! Sieh sie nicht an!

NARRABOTH

Yes, she'll pass by us here. Ja, sie kommt auf uns zu.

PAGE

Don't stare at her! Heed what I say! Ich bitte dich, sieh sie nicht an!

NARRABOTH

She's like a fugitive dove at nightfall. Sie ist wie eine verirrte Taube.
[5]

Scene Two. *Salome enters, excited.*

SALOME

I will not stay there. I cannot stay there. Ich will nicht bleiben. Ich kann nicht
But why, why should Herod always bleiben. Warum sieht mich der Tetrarch
stare at me thus, with his repulsive [6] fortwährend so an mit seinen
mole's eyes, under those flickering Maulwurfsaugen unter den zuckenden
eyelids? It's so curious when my own Lidern? Es ist seltsam, dass der Mann
mother's husband looks at me so. Out [7] meiner Mutter mich so ansieht. Wie süss
here the air is so sweet. Here I breathe [5] ist hier die Luft. Hier kann ich atmen.
freely ... In there are gathered Jews [3] Da drinnen sitzen Juden aus Jerusalem,
from old Jerusalem, who decry their die einander über ihre närrischen
neighbours' foolish rites and tear each Gebräuche in Stücke reissen.
other to shreds and tatters. Secretive, Schweigsame, list'ge Egypter und
crafty Egyptians, and ill mannered brutale, ungeschlachte Römer mit ihrer
acrimonious Romans with their barbaric plumpen Sprache. O, wie ich diese
voices. Oh, how I do detest those Römer hasse!
Romans!

PAGE

Terrible things will happen. Why d'you Schreckliches wird geschehn. Warum
stare at her like that? [7] siehst du sie so an?

SALOME

How lovely just to watch the moon. She [5] Wie gut ist's in den Mond zu sehn. Er
hovers like a huge silvery blossom, cool ist wie eine silberne Blume, kühl und
and chaste. She has the beauty of a [1] keusch. Ja, wie die Schönheit einer
virgin for ever undefiled. [5] Jungfrau, die rein geblieben ist.

VOICE OF JOKANAAN

Learn that the Lord is approaching, the [4c] Siehe, der Herr ist gekommen, des
Son of Man is near us. [4a] Menschen Sohn ist nahe.

SALOME

Who spoke then, who was that calling [5] Wer war das, der hier gerufen hat?
out?

SECOND SOLDIER

Princess, that was the Prophet. [4c] Der Prophet, Prinzessin.

Ah, so he's there! He, of whom Herod's [1] Ach, der Prophet. Der, vor dem der
so frightened.   Tetrarch Angst hat.

SECOND SOLDIER

Of that, the likes of us know nothing, [5a] Wir wissen davon nichts, Prinzessin. Es
but that was the prophet Jokanaan who   war der Prophet Jochanaan, der hier
cried out.   rief.

NARRABOTH
(*to Salome*)

Is it your wish I should have them go   [1] Beliebt es Euch, dass ich eure Sänfte
and bring your litter, Princess? The   [2] holen lasse, Prinzessin? Die Nacht ist
gardens look enchanting.   schön im Garten.

SALOME

He makes foul accusations that concern [7] Er sagt schreckliche Dinge über meine
my mother, does he not?   Mutter, nicht wahr?

SECOND SOLDIER

Princess, what he says makes no sense [5a] Wir verstehen nie, was er sagt,
to us here.   Prinzessin.

SALOME

Yes, he makes foul accusations   Ja, er sagt schreckliche Dinge über sie.
concerning her.

A SLAVE
(*entering*)

The Tetrarch bids me ask the Princess if   Prinzessin, der Tetrarch ersucht Euch,
she would join the feast again.   wieder zum Fest hinein zu gehn.

SALOME
(*passionately*)

I'll not go inside, there.   [7] Ich will nicht hinein gehn.
                                                       Exit slave.
This prophet of yours is old and grey.   [5] Ist dieser Prophet ein alter Mann?

NARRABOTH
(*more persistent*)

But Princess it would be better to go   [1] Prinzessin, es wäre besser hinein
inside. Allow me to lead you back there.   zu gehn. Gestattet, dass ich Euch führe!

SALOME
(*emphatically*)
[5]

This prophet of yours is old and grey?   Ist dieser Prophet ein alter Mann?
                                   [1a]

FIRST SOLDIER

No, this prophet is still quite young.   Nein, Prinzessin, er ist ganz jung.

VOICE OF JOKANAAN

Palestine, think not of rejoicing that the [4a] Jauche nicht, du Land Palästina, weil der
rod which smote you by His word is   Stab dessen, der dich schlug, gebrochen
now destroyed. For, from the seed of the [6] ist. Denn aus dem Samen der Schlange
serpent, shall a basilisk flourish; its brood   wird ein Basilisk kommen und seine
shall then devour the birds of the forest.   Brut wird die Vögel verschlingen.

SALOME

How strangely he's talking. I'd rather   [5] Welch seltsame Stimme! Ich möchte mit
like to speak with him.   ihm sprechen.

SECOND SOLDIER

Oh, Princess, but the Tetrarch's long   [4c] Prinzessin, der Tetrarch duldet nicht, decreed that none shall speak with this man. He has said that even the High Priest in person is not to speak with him.

dass irgend wer mit ihm spricht. Er hat selbst dem Hohen-priester verboten, mit ihm zu sprechen.

SALOME

I tell you I wish to speak with him.   [5] Ich wünsche mit ihm zu sprechen.

SECOND SOLDIER

But Princess, that is impossible.   Es ist unmöglich, Prinzessin.

SALOME
(still more passionate)

I tell you I'd speak with him.   [5] Ich will mit ihm sprechen!
Go, bring up the prophet, out here!   Bringt diesen Propheten heraus!

SECOND SOLDIER

We can't do that, Princess.   Wir dürfen nicht, Prinzessin.

SALOME
(approaching the cistern and looking down)

How dark it all looks below. Oh, how terrible to live there in such a black, gloomy cavern. It looks so like a grave . . .

Wie schwarz es da drunten ist! Es muss schrecklich sein, in so einer schwarzen Höhle zu leben . . . Es ist wie eine Gruft . . .

(wildly)

You heard what I said? Bring me the prophet at once! I want him out here!   [5] Habt ihr nicht gehört? Bringt den Propheten heraus! Ich möchte ihn sehn.

FIRST SOLDIER

No Princess, we cannot obey the order you have given.

Prinzessin, wir dürfen nicht tun, was ihr von uns begehrt.

SALOME
(noticing Narraboth)

Ah!   [5] Ah!

PAGE

What will happen now? I'm sure something terrible is near.

O, was wird geschehn? Ich weiss, es wird Schreckliches geschehn.

SALOME
(going up to Narraboth and speaking softly and excitedly)

You will do this for me, Narraboth, won't you? I've always treated you kindly. You'll do this thing for me. I want to take a look at this strange, outlandish prophet, for people have been saying so much about him. I gather Herod goes in fear of him.

[5] Du wirst das für mich tun, Narraboth,
[1a] nicht wahr? Ich war dir immer gewogen.
[2] Du wirst das für mich tun. Ich möchte
[5, 1a] ihn blos sehn, diesen seltsamen Propheten. Die Leute haben soviel von ihm gesprochen. Ich glaube, der Tetrarch hat Angst vor ihm.

NARRABOTH

But the Tetrarch has firmly given orders that none of us may open the grille above that cistern.

Der Tetrarch hat es ausdrücklich
[2] verboten, dass irgend wer den Deckel zu diesem Brunnen aufhebt.

SALOME

You will do this for me, Narraboth.   Du wirst das für mich tun, Narraboth,
(very hastily)
Tomorrow they'll take me in my litter [1a] und morgen, wenn ich in meiner Sänfte through the gateway where the idol makers stand; if you'll wait there,

an dem Torweg, wo die Götzenbilder stehn, vorbeikomme,
(always in a low voice)
I will throw a tiny flower for you as I'm [2] werde ich eine kleine Blume für dich passing, a tiny green flower.

fallen lassen, ein kleines grünes Blümchen.

31

NARRABOTH

But Princess, I cannot, I cannot!	Prinzessin, ich kann nicht, ich kann nicht!

SALOME
(*more positive*)

You will do this for me, Narraboth. You know you will do what I ask you. And then, at dawn, under my veil of scented muslin, you'll see my eyes upon you, Narraboth, you'll see that I'm looking, perhaps you'll see me smile at you. Look at me Narraboth, look at me. For you know too well you'll obey me, and do what I ask you. You know it well!	[1a] Du wirst das für mich tun, Narraboth. Du weisst, dass du das für mich tun wirst. Und morgen früh werde ich unter [2] den Muss'linschleiern dir einen Blick [1a] zuwerfen, Narraboth, ich werde dich ansehn, kann sein, ich werde dir zulächeln. Sieh mich an, Narraboth, sieh [2] mich an. Ah, wie gut du weisst, dass du tun wirst, um was ich dich bitte. Wie du es weisst!

(*forcibly*)

I know you'll not refuse!	[5] Ich weiss, du wirst das tun!

NARRABOTH
(*making a sign to the soldiers*)

Guards, let the prophet come up outside here ... for the Princess Salome wants to see this man.	Lasst den Propheten herauskommen ... [4c] die Prinzessin Salome wünscht ihn zu sehn.

SALOME
[5]

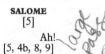

Ah!	Ah!
	[5, 4b, 8, 9]

Scene Three. *The Prophet comes out of the cistern. Salome, absorbed in his appearance, steps slowly back.*

JOKANAAN
(*with power*)
[4b]

Where is he, he, whose sins are now without number? Where is he, who, when the day comes, before the eyes of the people, dressed in a silver robe, will die at last. Call him here straightway, that he on this day may heed the voice of one who in the desert and in the houses of mighty kings proclaimed the Lord.	Wo ist er, dessen Sündenbecher jetzt voll ist? Wo ist er, der eines Tages im Angesicht alles Volkes in einem [8] Silbermantel sterben wird? Heisst ihn [4b] herkommen, auf dass er die Stimme Dessen höre, der in der Wüste und in den Häusern der Könige gekündet hat. [8]

SALOME

Of whom does he speak?	[5] Von wem spricht er?

NARRABOTH

No one knows the answer, Princess.	Niemand kann es sagen, Prinzessin.

JOKANAAN

Where is she who succumbed to the lust of her body, who, when she beheld those painted scenes of naked warriors, sent her messengers into Babylonia?	[4b] Wo ist sie, die sich hingab der Lust ihrer [10] Augen, die gestanden hat vor buntgemalten Männerbildern und Gesandte in's Land der Chaldäer schickte?

SALOME
(*whispering*)

He speaks about my mother.	Er spricht von meiner Mutter.

NARRABOTH
(impetuously)

No, no, Princess.	Nein, nein, Prinzessin.

SALOME
(faintly)

Yes, he speaks about my mother.	Ja, er spricht von meiner Mutter.

JOKANAAN

Where is she whom the chieftains of Assyria seduced? Where is she, she who did give herself to young Egyptian ambassadors, clad in finest linen, flaunting their gold and precious jewels, with their shields made of silver and their bodies like giants? Go, bid her rise up from the bed of her incest, from her couch of corruption, that she may attend the words of the prophet, who prepares the way of the Saviour, that she may now repent of her errors. And though she never repent, bid her come hear me, for the scourge of the Lord trembles in His hand.	[4b] Wo ist sie, die den Hauptleuten Assyriens sich gab? Wo ist sie, die sich den jungen Männern der Egypter gegeben hat, die in feinen Leinen und Hyacinthgesteinen prangen, deren Schilde von Gold sind und die Leiber [4c] wie Riesen? Geht, heisst sie aufsteh'n [8] vom Bett ihrer Greuel, vom Bett ihrer [4b] Blutschande, auf dass sie die Worte Dessen vernehme, der dem Herrn die [10] Wege bereitet, und ihre Missetaten bereue. Und wenn sie gleich nicht bereut, heisst sie herkommen, denn die Geissel des Herrn ist in seiner Hand.

SALOME

He is terrible. He is really terrible.	[11] Er ist schrecklich. Er ist wirklich schrecklich.

NARRABOTH

Do not stay here, Princess, I beg of you!	[2] Bleibt nicht hier, Prinzessin, ich bitte Euch!

SALOME

And his eyes are the most terrible thing of all. They're black as the fearsome caverns where the dragons linger! They shine like sombre lakes where some unearthly moonlight flickers. D'you you think that he will start to speak again?	Seine Augen sind von allem das [11] Schrecklichste. Sie sind wie die schwarzen Höhlen, wo die Drachen [1a] hausen! Sie sind wie schwarze Seen, aus denen irres Mondlicht flackert. Glaubt ihr, dass er noch einmal sprechen wird?

NARRABOTH
(still more excited)

Do not stay here, Princess, I beg of you, do not stay!	[2] Bleibt nicht hier, Prinzessin, ich bitte Euch, bleibt nicht hier!

SALOME

How pale and wan he looks! As though he were carved out of ivory. I'm sure he is chaste like the moon. His flesh must be cool, cool as ivory. I'd like to look closer at him.	[8] Wie abgezehrt er ist! Er ist wie ein Bildnis aus Elfenbein. Gewiss ist er [1a, 5] keusch wie der Mond. Sein Fleisch muss [11] sehr kühl sein, kühl wie Elfenbein. Ich möchte ihn näher beseh'n.

NARRABOTH

No, no, Princess.	[2] Nein, nein, Prinzessin.

SALOME

I must look closer at him.	[11, 1a] Ich muss ihn näher beseh'n.

NARRABOTH

Princess, Princess!	[2] Prinzessin, Prinzessin!

JOKANAAN

Who is this woman who stares	[1a, 8, 4a] Wer ist dies Weib, das mich ansieht? Ich

Above: Simon Estes as Jokanaan and Julia Migenes-Johnson as Salome at the Grand Théâtre, Geneva. Below: Gwyneth Jones as Salome with José van Dam as Jokanaan and Robin Leggate as Narraboth at Covent Garden (photo: Clive Barda)

at me? I'll not have her glances fixed
thus upon me. Just why does she stare
at me with those two eyes golden under
their shimmering eyelids? I know   [5, 10a]
not who she is. I do not wish to know
who she is. Bid her go! For I will not
speak to her.

will ihre Augen nicht auf mir haben.
Warum sieht sie mich so an, mit ihren
Goldaugen unter den gleissenden Lidern?
Ich weiss nicht, wer sie ist. Ich will
nicht wissen, wer sie ist. Heisst sie gehn!
Zu ihr will ich nicht sprechen.

SALOME

I am Salome, the daughter of   [5, 1a]
Herodias, and Princess of Judæa.

Ich bin Salome, die Tochter der
Herodias, Prinzessin von Judäa.

JOKANAAN

Away, daughter of Babylon! Do not
approach him the Lord has chosen. Your   [10]
own mother has corrupted the earth
with the wine of her orgies and the
burden of her wickedness cries to God.

Zurück, Tochter Babylons! Komm dem
Erwählten des Herrn nicht nahe! Deine
Mutter hat die Erde erfüllt mit dem
Wein ihrer Lüste, und das Unmass ihrer
Sünden schreit zu Gott.

SALOME

Speak on, Jokanaan, wondrous music   [10]
rings in my ears when you are speaking.   [9]

Sprich mehr, Jochanaan, deine Stimme
ist wie Musik in meinen Ohren.

NARRABOTH

Princess, Princess, Princess.   [2]

Prinzessin, Prinzessin, Prinzessin.

SALOME

Speak on, speak on, Jokanaan, and tell   [10]
me what you counsel.

Sprich mehr, sprich mehr, Jochanaan,
und sag' mir, was ich tun soll.

JOKANAAN

Daughter of Sodom, venture no nearer!   [10]
Instead go veil your face in token of
repentance, scatter ashes upon your
head, then go out in the desert and seek   [4b]
there the Son of Man!

Tochter Sodoms, komm mir nicht nahe!
Vielmehr bedecke dein Gesicht mit
einem Schleier, streue Asche auf deinen
Kopf, mach dich auf in die Wüste und
suche des Menschen Sohn!

SALOME

Who is that, the Son of Man? Is he as   [11]
fair as you Jokanaan?

Wer ist das, des Menschen Sohn? Ist er
so schön wie du, Jochanaan?

JOKANAAN

Leave me, I say! For there in that palace
I hear the rustling wings of death's dark
angel . . .

Weiche von mir! Ich höre die Flügel des
Todesengels im Palaste rauschen.

SALOME

Jokanaan!

Jochanaan!

NARRABOTH

Oh Princess, I beg you, go inside!   [10a , 2]

Prinzessin, ich flehe, geh' hinein!

SALOME

Jokanaan! Your body wakens my   [1a, 11]
desire, Jokanaan! Your flesh is white as   [9]
the lilies upon a meadow where the
scythe has never passed. Your flesh is
white as the snow on the hills of Judæa.
The flowers in the gardens of Arabia's
fabled Queen are not so white as your
flesh, not the flowers in the gardens of
Arabia's Queen, nor the footsteps of
dawn that waken the forest, nor the
breast of the moon upon the ocean.
Naught in this world is so white as your
flesh.

Jochanaan! Ich bin verliebt in deinen
Leib, Jochanaan! Dein Leib ist weiss wie
die Lilien auf einem Felde von der
Sichel nie berührt. Dein Leib ist weiss
wie der Schnee auf den Bergen Judäas.
Die Rosen im Garten von Arabiens
Königin sind nicht so weiss wie dein
Leib, nicht die Rosen im Garten der
Königin, nicht die Füsse der
Dämmerung auf den Blättern, nicht die
Brüste des Mondes auf dem Meere.
Nichts in der Welt ist so weiss wie dein
Leib.

35

(tenderly)

Let my gentle fingers touch [8, 10a, 1a] Lass mich ihn berühren deinen Leib.
your flesh.

JOKANAAN
(with great excitement)

Stand back, daughter of Babylon! [4b] Zurück, Tochter Babylons! Durch das
Womankind first brought Evil to the [5] Weib kam das Übel in die Welt. Sprich
world. Speak not to me, for I shall not [4a] nicht zu mir. Ich will dich nicht
hear you! The only voice I hear is the [4b] anhör'n! Ich höre nur auf die Stimme
voice of the Lord my Creator. des Herrn meines Gottes.

SALOME

Your flesh is horrible. It looks like [8, 11] Dein Leib ist grauenvoll. Er ist wie der
the flesh of a leper himself. It shines as Leib eines Aussätzigen. Er ist wie eine
foul as a whitened wall, which vipers getünchte Wand, wo Nattern gekrochen
have stained with slime, evil as a sind, wie eine getünchte Wand, wo
whitened wall where the scorpions have Skorpione ihr Nest gebaut. Er ist wie ein
built their nests. It gleams like a übertünchtes Grab voll widerlicher
whitened sepulchre that hides so many Dinge. Er ist grässlich, dein Leib ist
horrors. It is hideous, your flesh is [11, 10a] grässlich. In dein Haar bin ich verliebt,
hideous. I'm enamoured of your [5] Jochanaan. Dein Haar ist wie
hair, Jokanaan. Your hair is like the vine Weintrauben, wie Büschel schwarzer
harvest that hangs in swarthy clusters in Trauben an den Weinstöcken Edoms.
the vineyards of Edom. Your hair is like [7] Dein Haar ist wie die Cedern, die
the cedars, the towering cedars of grossen Cedern von Libanon, die den
Lebanon, hiding lions and robbers in [5] Löwen und Räubern Schatten spenden.
their shadows. The long black nights of Die langen schwarzen Nächte, wenn der
winter, when the moon hides her face Mond sich verbirgt, wenn die Sterne
and the stars are frightened, are not so [7] bangen, sind nicht so schwarz wie dein
black as your hair. No silent forest . . . Haar. Des Waldes Schweigen . . . Nichts
Naught in the world is so black as your in der Welt ist so schwarz wie dein
hair. Oh, let me caress your hair. [11, 10a , 1a] Haar. Lass mich es berühren dein Haar.

JOKANAAN

Away, daughter of Sodom! [5] Zurück, Tochter Sodoms!
Do not touch me, I say! nor dare [4b] Berühre mich nicht! Entweihe nicht den
profane the house of the Lord, my Tempel des Herrn, meines Gottes!
Creator!

SALOME

Your hair is hideous, besmirched [8, 10a, 5] Dein Haar ist grässlich! Es starrt von
with dust and rubble. It looks more like Staub und Unrat. Es ist wie eine
a crown of briars they've set upon your Dornenkrone auf deinen Kopf gesetzt.
head. It looks like a tangle of serpents Es ist wie ein Schlangenknoten
entwined in knots round your neck. gewickelt um deinen Hals. Ich liebe dein
Your hair does not charm me. Haar nicht.

(with the utmost passion)

It's your mouth that I desire, Jokanaan. [4b] Deinen Mund begehre ich, Jochanaan.
Your mouth is like a scarlet band upon a Dein Mund ist wie ein Scharlachband
tower of ivory, or like the pomegranate an einem Turm von Elfenbein. Er ist
fruit a silver knife has severed in two. wie ein Granatapfel, den ein
But the pomegranate blossoms in the Silbermesser zerteilt. Die Granatapfel-
gardens at Tyrus, ruddier than roses, are blüten in den Gärten von Tyrus,
not so red. The bloodthirsty fanfares of glüh'nder als Rosen, sind nicht so rot.
the trumpets that proclaim some royal Die roten Fanfaren der Trompeten, die
triumph, while the enemy cowers in das Nah'n von Kön'gen künden und vor
terror, are not so red as your scarlet denen der Feind erzittert, sind nicht so
mouth. Your mouth is redder than the rot wie dein roter Mund. Dein Mund ist
bare feet of men who tread the vines röter als die Füsse der Männer, die den
gathered in the wine press. It is redder Wein stampfen in der Kelter. Er ist röter
than the feet of the doves that nest in als die Füsse der Tauben, die in den
the temple towers. Your mouth is red as Tempeln wohnen. Dein Mund ist wie
a coral branch from the dim twilight ein Korallenzweig in der Dämm'rung
sea, red as purple from the valleys of des Meers, wie der Purpur in den

Moab, the purple of emperors . . .

(beside herself)

Naught in the world is so red as your mouth. Will you not let me kiss your mouth?

JOKANAAN

(low, in voiceless horror)

Never! Daughter of Babylon! Daughter of Sodom . . . No, never!

SALOME

I long for your mouth's kisses, Jokanaan, [12]
I long for your mouth's kisses.

NARRABOTH

(in the greatest anguish and despair)

Princess, Princess, you lovely garden of [2] scented myrrh, you, the dove of all the turtle doves, you must not look at him. Do not say such things to this man. I [1a] cannot bear to hear them . . .

SALOME

I long for your mouth's kisses, Jokanaan. [12]
I long for your mouth's kisses . . . [2, 1a, 10a]

Naraboth kills himself with a knife and falls between Salome and Jokanaan.
Let me kiss your mouth, Jokanaan. [12, 5]

JOKANAAN

Are you not frightened, daughter [4b, 5a]
of Herodias?

SALOME

Let me kiss your mouth, I say, [12]
Jokanaan!

JOKANAAN

Daughter of a harlot, there lives but one [4b]
man who can save you now. Go, seek
Him. Seek Him! [8, 12]

(fervently)

He's seated in a vessel on the sea of [13]
Galilæa and preaches to His disciples.

(most solemnly)

Kneel down, there, by the shore of [12, 4b]
the sea, call His name, His holy name of
Saviour. When He approaches (and He
comes to all who call upon Him),
prostrate yourself before His presence,
pray that He then may grant you [8]
forgiveness.

SALOME

(as though in despair)

Let me kiss your mouth, I say,
Jokanaan.

JOKANAAN

Be accursed, daughter of a shameless [8]
incestuous mother, be accursed. [11, 12]

Gruben von Moab, der Purpur der Könige . . .

Nichts in der Welt ist so rot wie dein Mund. Lass mich ihn küssen deinen Mund.

JOKANAAN

Niemals, Tochter Babylons, Tochter Sodoms! Niemals!

SALOME

Ich will deinen Mund küssen, Jochanaan. Ich will deinen Mund küssen.

NARRABOTH

Prinzessin, Prinzessin, die wie ein Garten von Myrrhen ist, die die Taube aller Tauben ist, sieh diesen Mann nicht an. Sprich nicht solche Worte zu ihm. Ich kann es nicht ertragen . . .

SALOME

Ich will deinen Mund küssen, Jochanaan. Ich will deinen Mund küssen . . .

Lass mich deinen Mund küssen, Jochanaan!

JOKANAAN

Wird dir nicht bange, Tochter Herodias?

SALOME

Lass mich deinen Mund küssen, Jochanaan!

JOKANAAN

Tochter der Unzucht, es lebt nur Einer, der dich retten kann. Geh, such' ihn. Such' ihn!

Er ist in einem Nachen auf dem See von Galiläa und redet zu seinen Jüngern.

Knie nieder am Ufer des Sees, ruf ihn an. Und rufe ihn beim Namen. Wenn er zu dir kommt, und er kommt zu allen, die ihn rufen, dann bücke dich zu seinen Füssen, dass er dir deine Sünden vergebe.

SALOME

Lass mich deinen Mund küssen, Jochanaan!

JOKANAAN

Sei verflucht, Tochter der blut-schänderischen Mutter. Sei verflucht!

Let me kiss your mouth, I say,
Jokanaan.

Lass mich deinen Mund küssen,
Jochanaan!

JOKANAAN

No, I will not look at you. You are
accursed, Salome. You are accursed. You
are accursed. You are accursed.

[4c] Ich will dich nicht ansehn. Du bist
verflucht, Salome. Du bist verflucht. Du
[12] bist verflucht.

He goes back down into the cistern.
[8, 11, 9, 10a, 12, 4b, 10b, 14a, 14b]

large inst. passage

Scene Four. *Herod enters hastily, followed by Herodias.*

HEROD
[3, 15]

Where is Salome? Where is the
Princess? And then, why did she not
rejoin the feast when I'd ordered her to
do so? Ah, there she is!

Wo ist Salome? Wo ist die Prinzessin?
Warum kam sie nicht wieder zum
Bankett, wie ich ihr befohlen hatte? Ah!
[16] Da ist sie!

HERODIAS

Your eyes never leave her. You should
not stare at her so!

[17] Du sollst sie nicht ansehn. Fortwährend
siehst du sie an!

HEROD
[16]

How peculiar the moon's looking! Is
she not a strange, curious sight? She has
the face of a wild, half-witted wench
who looks for lovers everywhere . . . or
one reeling thro' the clouds like a
drunken creature . . .

[15] Wie der Mond heute Nacht aussieht! Ist
es nicht ein seltsames Bild? Es sieht aus,
wie ein wahnwitziges Weib, das überall
[16] nach Buhlen sucht . . . wie ein
betrunkenes Weib, das durch Wolken
taumelt.

HERODIAS

No, the moon looks like the moon, just
as usual. Let's go back inside now.

Nein, der Mond ist wie der Mond, das
ist alles. Wir wollen hineingehn.

[17]

HEROD

I'll stay here, I tell you. Mannasseh, lay
carpets on the ground! Bring some
torches out! My guests and I will drink
more wine outside here. Ah, I have
slipped on something. But this is blood I
slipped on, and that's an evil omen. Why
should there be blood? And this dead
body? Then who can this dead man be?
Yes, who is this dead man? I don't wish
to see.

Ich will hier bleiben. Mannassah, leg
Teppiche hierher! Zündet Fackeln an!
Ich will noch Wein mit meinen Gästen
[18] trinken. Ah, ich bin ausgeglitten. Ich bin
in Blut getreten, das ist ein böses
Zeichen. Warum ist hier Blut? Und
dieser Tote? Wer ist dieser Tote hier?
Wer ist dieser Tote? Ich will ihn nicht
sehn.

FIRST SOLDIER

That man is our captain, sir.

Es ist unser Hauptmann, Herr.

HEROD

I myself did not command anyone here
to kill him.

Ich erliess keinen Befehl, dass er getötet
werde.

FIRST SOLDIER

He killed himself, a while since, sir.

Er hat sich selbst getötet, Herr.

HEROD

That is most curious. this handsome
Syrian still looked so young. I remember

[1a] Das scheint mir seltsam. Der junge
Syrier, er war sehr schön. Ich erinn're

38

now. I saw all those languishing glances, he bestowed upon the Princess. Take him off.

They take away the body.

It's so cold here, there's a wind . . . Is there a wind?

HERODIAS
(*dryly*)

No, there's no wind.

HEROD

I swear to you there is a wind and I can hear something stirring, like the rustling of mighty pinnions. You hear that sound?

HERODIAS

I hear no sound.

HEROD

Ah! now I cannot hear it. Oh, but I really heard a noise, as if the wind were moaning. Now all is quiet. Hark! Do you not hear? The rustling of mighty pinnions . . .

HERODIAS

You are ill. Let's go back inside now.

HEROD

No, I'm not ill, but it is your daughter who's sick and ailing. Never has she looked so pale before.

HERODIAS

I've told you many times that you should not stare at her.

HEROD

Pour out wine for me! Salome, come drink wine with me, this is marvellous wine. Caesar sent it to me himself. Come and dip you little lips in this wine. Your own little rosy lips, then I'll drain the goblet empty.

SALOME

I am not thirsty, Tetrarch.

HEROD

Listen how she replies to me, she, who is your daughter!

HERODIAS

She's quite right. Must you leer at her all the time?

HEROD

Bring me some fruit. Salome, come, eat with me some of this fruit here. The bite of your delightful pearly teeth tearing the fruit fills me with joy. Bite just a little piece, just a morsel from off this fruit, then I will eat what is left myself.

[2]
[5] mich, ich sah seine schmachtenden Augen, wenn er Salome ansah. Fort mit ihm.

Es ist kalt hier. Es weht ein Wind . . . Weht nicht ein Wind?

Nein, es weht kein Wind.

Ich sage Euch: es weht ein Wind, und in der Luft hör' ich etwas, wie das Rauschen [8] von mächt'gen Flügeln. Hört ihr es nicht?

Ich höre nichts.

[17] Jetzt höre ich es nicht mehr. Aber ich habe es gehört, es war das Wehn des Windes. Es ist vorüber. Horch! Hört Ihr [8] es nicht? Das Rauschen von mächt'gen Flügeln . . .

Du bist krank, wir wollen hineingehn.

[18] Ich bin nicht krank, aber deine Tochter [16] ist krank zu Tode. Niemals hab' ich sie [5] so blass gesehn.

Ich habe dir gesagt, du sollst sie nicht ansehn.

[17, 5] Schenkt mir Wein ein! Salome, komm, trink Wein mit mir, einen köstlichen Wein. Cäsar selbst hat ihn mir geschickt. [1a] Tauche deine kleinen Lippen hinein. Deine kleinen roten Lippen, dann will ich den Becher leeren.

Ich bin nicht durstig, Tetrarch.

Hörst du, wie sie mir antwortet, diese deine Tochter?

Sie hat Recht. Warum starrst du sie immer an?

Bringt reife Früchte! Salome, komm, iss mit mir von diesen Früchten. Den [19] Abdruck deiner kleinen, weissen Zähne in einer Frucht seh' ich so gern. Beiss nur ein wenig ab. Nur ein wenig von dieser Frucht, dann will ich essen' was übrig ist.

39

SALOME

I am not hungry, Tetrarch.

Ich bin nicht hungrig, Tetrarch.

HEROD

You see how your precious little daughter has been brought up!

Du siehst, wie du diese deine Tochter erzogen hast!

HERODIAS

Both my daughter and I come of an ancient royal line. Your father was a camel driver. Your father was a thief and a bandit, furthermore.

Meine Tochter und ich stammen aus königlichem Blut. Dein Vater war Kameltreiber, dein Vater war ein Dieb und ein Räuber obendrein.

HEROD

Salome, come, come here to me. Your own mother's throne shall be yours this evening.

Salome, komm, setz dich zu mir. Du [5] sollst auf dem Thron deiner Mutter sitzen.

SALOME

I am not weary, Tetrarch.

[1a, 14a] Ich bin nicht müde, Tetrarch.

HERODIAS

You see how she respects you.

Du siehst, wie sie dich achtet.

HEROD

Bring me — what is it I need? I seem to have forgotten. Ah! Ah! I remember now —

[5, 14a] Bringt mir — was wünsche ich denn? Ich habe es vergessen. Ah! Ah! Ich erinn're mich —

THE VOICE OF JOKANAAN

See, the time is upon us, the day of which I spoke is near.

[4a] Sieh, die Zeit ist gekommen, der Tag von dem ich sprach, ist da.

HERODIAS

Stop him talking! That man there insults me!

Heiss' ihn schweigen! Dieser Mensch beschimpft mich!

HEROD

It was not against you he spoke. Furthermore he is a prophet of renown.

Er hat nichts gegen dich gesagt. Überdies ist er ein sehr grosser Prophet.

HERODIAS

I have no faith in these prophets. As for you, you're afraid of him!

Ich glaube nicht an Propheten. Aber du, [15] du hast Angst vor ihm!

HEROD

I'm afraid of no one alive.

[5a] Ich habe vor niemandem Angst.

HERODIAS

I still repeat, you're afraid of him. Why not hand him over to the Jews out there? They've been screaming for months to get him.

[15] Ich sage dir, du hast Angst vor ihm. Warum lieferst du ihn nicht den Juden aus, die seit Monaten nach ihm schreien?

FIRST JEW

That's very true, it would be better if you'd give him into our keeping!

Wahrhaftig, Herr, es wäre besser, ihn in uns're Hände zu geben.

HEROD

Enough of this! I'll never surrender him into your keeping. For he's a holy man. He is a man whom God has looked on.

[15] Genug davon! Ich werde ihn nicht in eure Hände geben. Er ist ein heil'ger Mann. Er ist ein Mann, der Gott geschaut hat.

(Banquet)

FIRST JEW

That can't be true. For since the prophet Elijah, no man has seen our God. He was the last man to whom God himself appeared. Today our God appears to no one. God is hiding. That's why these fearful evils ravage the land we live in — fearful evils.

[3] Das kann nicht sein. Seit dem Propheten Elias hat niemand Gott gesehn. Er war der letzte, der Gott von Angesicht geschaut. In unser'n Tagen zeigt sich Gott nicht. Gott verbirgt sich. Darum ist grosses Übel über das Land gekommen, grosses Übel.

SECOND JEW

But no one is certain that Elijah did in fact really see the Lord. It's far more likely that it was His passing shadow that he saw.

In Wahrheit weiss niemand, ob Elias in der Tat Gott gesehen hat. Möglicherweise war es nur der Schatten Gottes, was er sah.

THIRD JEW

God is at no time ever hidden. He showeth Himself at all times and in all creation. God is in evil, even as in perfection.

Gott ist zu keiner Zeit verborgen. Er zeigt sich zu allen Zeiten und an allen Orten. Gott ist im Schlimmen ebenso wie im Guten.

FOURTH JEW

You should not talk such nonsense, for that is a highly dangerous dogma from Alexandria. And the Greeks there are Gentiles.

Du solltest das nicht sagen, es ist eine sehr gefährliche Lehre aus Alexandria. Und die Griechen sind Heiden.

FIFTH JEW

No one can tell us how God works. All his ways are so mysterious. We can but bow down our heads and obey His wise commandments, for God has much power.

Niemand kann sagen, wie Gott wirkt. Seine Wege sind sehr dunkel. Wir können nur unser Haupt unter seinen Willen beugen, denn Gott ist sehr stark.

FIRST JEW

You speak the truth there. Indeed, God is righteous, but it is certain that this man here has not seen God himself. For since the prophet Elijah, no man has seen our God.

Du sagst die Wahrheit. Fürwahr, Gott ist furchtbar. Aber was diesen Menschen angeht, der hat Gott nie gesehn. Seit dem Propheten Elias hat niemand Gott gesehn.

SECOND JEW

But none is certain that Elijah did in fact really see our God.

In Wahrheit weiss niemand, ob Elias in der Tat Gott gesehen hat.

FIRST JEW

He was the last man, *etc.*

Er war der letzte, *usw.*

SECOND JEW

But no one is certain that Elijah did in fact, *etc.* God is righteous, He breaks the strongest to pieces. The strongest and the weakest to Him are all alike. It's far more likely that it was His passing shadow.

In Wahrheit weiss niemand, ob Elias in der Tat Gott gesehen hat. *usw.* Gott ist furchtbar, er bricht den Starken in Stükke, den Starken wie den Schwachen, denn jeder gilt ihm gleich.

THIRD JEW

God is at no time ever hidden. *etc.*

Gott ist zu keiner Zeit verborgen. *usw.*

FOURTH JEW
(to the Third)

You should not really say that. They've

Du solltest das nicht sagen. Sie sind

not been circumcised either. No one can tell us how God works, for God has much power. *etc.*

nicht einmal beschnitten. Niemand kann sagen, wie Gott wirkt, denn Gott ist sehr stark. *usw.*

FIFTH JEW

No one can tell us how God works. *etc.* It may be that the doctrines all the world praises are evil and the doctrines others call evil are righteous. Our knowledge is pitiful. Our knowledge is pitiful, yes, pitiful . . .

Niemand kann sagen, wie Gott wirkt. *usw.* Es kann sein, dass die Dinge, die wir gut nennen, sehr schlimm sind, und die Dinge, die wir schlimm nennen, sehr gut sind. Wir wissen von nichts etwas. Wir wissen von nichts etwas, von nichts etwas . . .

HERODIAS
(to Herod, bursting out)

Stop their chatter.

Heiss sie schweigen.

SECOND JEW

It's far more likely that it was His passing shadow . . .

Möglicherweise war es nur der Schatten Gottes . . .

HERODIAS

They bore me to death!

Sie langweilen mich!

HEROD

I've heard it said by people here, that Jokanaan is quite clearly your own prophet Elijah.

[15] Doch hab ich davon sprechen hören, Jochanaan sei in Wahrheit euer Prophet Elias.

FIRST JEW

That cannot be. Since the time of our great prophet Elijah, far more than three hundred years have counted.

Das kann nicht sein, seit den Tagen des Propheten Elias sind mehr als dreihundert Jahre vergangen.

FIRST NAZARENE

I'm quite certain that that is the prophet Elijah there.

Mir ist sicher, dass er der Prophet Elias ist.

FIRST JEW

That cannot be. Since the time of our great prophet Elijah, far more than three hundred years have been counted . . .

Das kann nicht sein. Seit den Tagen des Propheten Elias sind mehr als dreihundert Jahre vergangen . . .

SECOND, THIRD, FOURTH AND FIFTH JEWS

That's not true, no, he can't be the prophet Elijah.

Keineswegs, er ist nicht der Prophet Elias.

HERODIAS

Stop their chatter!

Heiss sie schweigen!

THE VOICE OF JOKANAAN

Brothers, the day is near us, the day of the Lord. Far upon the distant mountains, I hear the footsteps of Him who'll be the Saviour of man.

[4b] Siehe, der Tag ist nahe, der Tag des Herrn, und ich höre auf den Bergen die Schritte Dessen, der sein wird der Erlöser der Welt.

HEROD

What does that mean then, 'Be the Saviour of Man'?

Was soll das heissen, der Erlöser der Welt?

FIRST NAZARENE
(emphatically)

The Messiah is among us.

Der Messias ist gekommen.

FIRST JEW
(screaming)

The Messiah is not among us. Der Messias ist nicht gekommen.

FIRST NAZARENE

He is among us and where he passes [13] Er ist gekommen, und allenthalben tu
works great wonders. er Wunder.

(very quietly)

For at a wedding in Galilæa He turned Bei einer Hochzeit in Galiläa hat er
water into wine, one morning. Two Wasser in Wein verwandelt. Er heilte
lepers were cured instantly at zwei Aussätzige von Capernaum.
Capernaum.

SECOND NAZARENE

His hands barely touched them. Durch blosses Berühren!

FIRST NAZARENE

Some blind men also were healed. He Er hat auch Blinde geheilt. Man hat i
was seen upon a mountain, speaking low auf einem Berge im Gespräch mit
with angels from Heaven! Engeln gesehn!

HERODIAS

Ho ho! I have no faith in wonders, I've Oho! Ich glaube nicht an Wunder,
seen too many of those in my time! ich habe ihrer zu viele gesehn!

FIRST NAZARENE

The daughter of Jairus by His power Die Tochter des Jairus hat er von den
was brought back to life. Toten erweckt.

HEROD
(frightened)

What, He brings the dead to life? Wie, er erweckt die Toten?

SECOND AND FIRST NAZARENES

Ah, yes, brings the dead to life. Jawohl. Er erweckt die Toten.

HEROD

I forbid this man such a thing. It would Ich verbiete ihm, das zu tun. Es wäre
be frightful if the dead came back to [4b] schrecklich, wenn die Toten
plague us! Where is this man today? wiederkämen! Wo ist der Mann zur
  Zeit?

FIRST NAZARENE

Sir, He is everywhere, but it is not easy Herr, er ist überall, aber es ist schwer,
to find Him. ihn zu finden.

HEROD

This man must be apprehended. Der Mann muss gefunden werden.

SECOND NAZARENE

They say He's in Samaria now, at this Es heisst, in Samaria weile er jetzt.
time.

FIRST NAZARENE

He left Samaria at dawn the other Vor ein paar Tagen verliess er Samaria
morning; I fancy that you can find Him ich glaube, im Augenblick ist er in der
on the outskirts of Jerusalem. Nähe von Jerusalem.

HEROD

Well then, I forbid this man to bring the So hört: ich verbiete ihm, die Toten zu
dead to life! erwecken!

THE VOICE OF JOKANAAN

Of this lascivious woman here, this daughter of Babylon, thus says the Lord our God:	O über dieses geile Weib, die Tochter Babylons. So spricht der Herr, unser Gott:

HEROD

It would be terrible if the dead came back to plague us!	Es müsste schrecklich sein, wenn die Toten wiederkämen!

HERODIAS
(furiously)

Command him to be silent!	Befiehl ihm, er soll schweigen!

THE VOICE OF JOKANAAN

Men shall soon rebel against the dissolute woman, they shall take up stones and stone her in their multitudes!	[4b] Eine Menge Menschen wird sich gegen sie sammeln, und sie werden Steine nehmen und sie steinigen!

HERODIAS

You heard him, he's outrageous!	Wahrhaftig, es ist schändlich!

THE VOICE OF JOKANAAN

The warrior chiefs shall gather round, and with their swords they shall pierce her, and with their many pointed shields they shall crush her!	[4b] Die Kriegshauptleute werden sie mit ihren Schwertern durchbohren, sie werden sie mit ihren Schilden zermalmen!

HERODIAS

Keep him quiet! Stop his yelling!	Er soll schweigen, er soll schweigen!

THE VOICE OF JOKANAAN

This must be, so that all of this evil shall be uprooted, so that I shall teach the race of women never to venture on her path of corruption!	Es ist so, dass ich alle Verruchtheit austilgen werde, dass ich alle Weiber [10] lehren werde, nicht auf den Wegen ihrer Greuel zu wandeln!

HERODIAS

You hear what he says against me? You'd let this man thus defame her who is your wife?	[10b]Du hörst, was er gegen mich sagt, du duldest es, dass er die schmähe, die dein Weib ist?

HEROD

He did not refer to you by name.	Er hat deinen Namen nicht genannt.

THE VOICE OF JOKANAAN
(very solemnly)

The day is near, the sun shall then be veiled in darkness like a sombre shroud. And the moon shall seem as of blood, and the stars of the Heavens shall fall on the earth about us, like shrivelling figs from the fig-tree branch. The day is near when the kings of the earth all shall tremble.	[8] Es kommt ein Tag, da wird die Sonne finster werden wie ein schwarzes Tuch. Und der Mond wird werden wie Blut, und die Sterne des Himmels werden zur Erde fallen wie unreife Feigen vom Feigenbaum. Es kommt ein Tag, wo die Kön'ge der Erde erzittern.

HERODIAS

Ah! Ah! That prophet there babbles like a drunken man . . . What a disgraceful noise he is making, I can't stand it! I find his voice quite hateful. [8, 17] Command him to be silent.	Ha, ha! Dieser Prophet schwatzt wie ein Betrunkener . . . aber ich kann den Klang seiner Stimme nicht ertragen, ich hasse seine Stimme. Befiehl ihm, er soll schweigen.

HEROD

Dance for me, Salome.

[5a] Tanz für mich, Salome!

HERODIAS
(vehemently)

I will not have her dance tonight.

Ich will nicht haben, dass sie tanzt.

SALOME
(quietly)

But I'm not in the mood for dancing Tetrarch.

Ich habe keine Lust zu tanzen, Tetrarch.

HEROD

Salome, daughter of Herodias, dance for me!

[5a] Salome, Tochter der Herodias, tanz für mich!

SALOME

I will not dance here, Tetrarch.

Ich will nicht tanzen, Tetrarch.

HERODIAS

You see, how this girl obeys.

Du siehst, wie sie dir gehorcht!

THE VOICE OF JOKANAAN

A king shall sit enthroned in glory. He shall be clothed in robes of scarlet and purple. And the angel of God shall come to overthrow him. The worms of the darkness shall feed upon him.

[20] Er wird auf seinem Throne sitzen, er wird gekleidet sein in Scharlach und Purpur. Und der Engel des Herrn wird ihn darnieder schlagen. Er wird von den Würmern gefressen werden.

HEROD

Salome, Salome, dance for me, I beg of you. I am rather sad tonight, so dance for me. Salome, dance for me! If you will but dance for me, then you may have what ever you desire.

[5] Salome, Salome, tanz für mich, ich bitte dich. Ich bin traurig heute Nacht, drum tanz für mich! Salome, tanz für mich! Wenn du für mich tanzest, kannst du von mir begehren, was du willst.

(pressingly)

Your wishes shall be granted.

Ich werde es dir geben.

SALOME
(rising)

Do you really mean you will give me anything I may ask for, Tetrarch?

[1a] Willst du mir wirklich alles geben, was ich von dir begehre, Tetrarch?

HERODIAS

Do not dance, my dear daughter!

Tanze nicht, meine Tochter!

HEROD

Nothing, nothing you ask will be denied to you; though it be half of all my royal realm.

[20] Alles, alles, was du von mir begehren wirst; und wärs die Hälfte meines Königreichs.

SALOME

You swear it, Tetrarch?

Du schwörst es, Tetrarch?

HEROD

I swear it, Salome.

Ich schwör' es, Salome.

SALOME

By what token will you swear it, Tetrarch?

Wobei willst du das beschwören, Tetrarch?

HEROD

By my kingdom, by my own life, by gods I honour.

Bei meinem Leben, bei meiner Krone, bei meinen Göttern.

Do not dance, I implore you.

Tanze nicht, meine Tochter!

HEROD

O Salome, Salome, dance for me!

O Salome, Salome, tanz für mich!

SALOME

Remember the oath you've taken, Tetrarch.

Du hast einen Eid geschworen, Tetrarch.

HEROD

I shall keep the oath I've taken.

Ich habe einen Eid geschworen.

HERODIAS

No, my daughter, do not dance.

Meine Tochter, tanze nicht.

HEROD

Though it be half of all my royal realm. As a Queen you'd be fair to see, yes, surpassing fair.

[17] Und wär's die Hälfte meines Königreichs. Du wirst schön sein als Königin, unermesslich schön.

(shivering)

Ah! it's so cold here. There is an icy wind, and I'm hearing . . . Come, say, why do I hear that sound like the rustling of pinnions? Ah! It seems as if there's some gigantic bird of dusky plumage, hovering low above the terrace. Oh, why can't I see this bird up above me? Ah, these noises are frightening! An icy wind fans my face. No, I'm wrong, it is not cold, it is hot. Pour some water over my fingers, give me snow to swallow. Undo my cloak for me. Quick, quick, undo my cloak for me! But no, leave it! How my crown pinches. All these roses are like fire.

[20] Ah! Es ist kalt hier. Es weht ein eis'ger Wind, und ich höre . . . Warum höre ich
[8] in der Luft dieses Rauschen von Flügeln? Ah! Es ist doch so, als ob ein ungeheurer, schwarzer Vogel über der Terrasse schwebte? Warum kann ich ihn
[16] nicht sehn, diesen Vogel? Dieses Rauschen ist schrecklich. Es ist ein
[8] schneidender Wind. Aber nein, er ist
[5] nicht kalt, er ist heiss. Giesst mir Wasser über die Hände, gebt mir Schnee zu
[20] essen, macht mir den Mantel los. Schnell, schnell, macht mir den Mantel
[18] los! Doch nein! Lasst ihn! Dieser Kranz drückt mich. Diese Rosen sind wie Feuer.

He tears the wreath from his head and throws it on the table.

Ah, I breathe more freely . Now I feel happier.

[18, 5] Ah! Jetzt kann ich atmen. Jetzt bin ich glücklich.

(faintly)

Dance for me, I beg you, Salome.

Willst du für mich tanzen, Salome?

HERODIAS

There'll be no dancing. I forbid it!

Ich will nicht haben, dass sie tanze!

SALOME

I'll dance for you, Tetrarch.

[1a] Ich will für dich tanzen.

Female slaves bring ointments and the seven veils and take off Salome's sandals.

THE VOICE OF JOKANAAN

Who is this who from Edom comes, who is this who from Bosrah comes, he whose robe is coloured with purple, who by his beauty radiates power and glory, who comes here in all his shining splendour. Why are your garments bespattered with blood?

[4b] Wer ist Der, der von Edom kommt, wer ist Der, der von Bosra kommt, dessen Kleid mit Purpur gefärbt ist, der in der Schönheit seiner Gewänder leuchtet, der mächtig in seiner Grösse wandelt, warum ist dein Kleid mit Scharlach gefleckt?

HERODIAS

Let's go back inside now. His voice will drive me crazy, that is quite certain.

Wir wollen hineingehn. Die Stimme dieses Menschen macht mich wahnsinnig.

Above: Gwyneth Jones as Salome, San Francisco, 1987 (photo: David Powers). Below: Anja Silja as Salome, San Francisco, 1968 (photo: Carolyn Mason Jones)

(more and more fiercely)

I'll not allow my daughter to dance for you while that man carries on all the time. No, I will never see her dance while you leer at her in such a manner. In just a word, I will not let my daughter dance.	Ich will nicht haben, dass meine Tochter tanzt, während er immer dazwischen schreit. Ich will nicht haben, dass sie tanzt, während du sie auf solche Art ansiehst. Mit einem Wort: ich will nicht haben, dass sie tanzt.

HEROD

Do not rise against me, my royal Queen, for that will not help you. I'll not go back inside until she has danced here. Dance now, Salome, dance for me!	Steh nicht auf, mein Weib, meine Königin. Es wird dir nichts helfen, ich gehe nicht hinein, bevor sie getanzt hat. [5] Tanze Salome, tanz für mich!

HERODIAS

Do not dance, I forbid it!	[16, 14b] Tanze nicht, meine Tochter!

SALOME

I'm ready now, Tetrarch.	Ich bin bereit, Tetrarch.

Salome's Dance. [14a, 1, 5, 9, 8, 12, 2, 11, 7]

The musicians begin a wild dance. Salome stands motionless. Salome rises to her full height and makes a sign to the musicians. They subdue the wild rhythm instantly and lead on to a soft and swaying tune. Salome dances the Dance of the Seven Veils. At the climax of the dance Salome seems to faint for a moment, then she pulls herself together as if with new strength. [5, 1a, 14a] *Salome remains for an instant in a visionary attitude near the cistern where Jokanaan is kept prisoner, then she throws herself at Herod's feet.* [7]

HEROD

Ah, heavenly! Wonderful, wonderful!	[16] Ah! Herrlich! Wundervoll, wundervoll!

(to Herodias)

Well then, you see that she has danced, your fair daughter. Come here Salome, come here, you've earned your reward from me, you shall be royally rewarded. I'll give you any treasure that your heart desires. What must I give you, say!	Siehst du, sie hat für mich getanzt, deine Tochter. Komm her, Salome, komm her, du sollst deinen Lohn haben. Ich will dich königlich belohnen. Ich will dir alles geben, was dein Herz begehrt. Was willst du haben? Sprich!

SALOME
(sweetly)

I want them to bring me now upon a silver charger . . .	[11a] Ich möchte, dass sie mir gleich in einer Silberschüssel . . .

HEROD

Upon a silver charger . . . why surely, upon a silver charger . . . She is charming, no? And what shall they bring on a silver charger for your pleasure, enchanting, radiant, Salome, you the fairest jewel of all the maids of Judæa! Come, what must they bring upon a silver charger to you? Tell me now! What you may ask me, to you shall be given. For a King's treasures belong to you. What is it you would have me give you, Salome?	In einer Silberschüssel . . . Gewiss doch — in einer Silberschüssel . . . Sie ist reizend, nicht? Was ist's, das du in einer Silberschüssel haben möchtest, o süsse, schöne Salome, du, die schöner ist als alle Töchter Judäas? Was sollen sie dir in einer Silberschüssel bringen? Sag es mir! Was es auch sein mag, du sollst es erhalten. Meine Reichtümer gehören dir. Was ist es, das du haben möchtest, Salome?

[11a]
Salome rises.

SALOME
(smiling)

The head of Jokanaan.	Den Kopf des Jochanaan.

HEROD
(rising abruptly)

No, no! [15, 20] Nein, nein!

HERODIAS

Ah! You are inspired, my dear daughter, you are inspired.

Ah! das sagst du gut, meine Tochter. Das sagst du gut!

HEROD

No, no, Salome, that cannot be what you desire! Don't listen to the voice of your mother. She always gave you bad advice. Pay no heed to her.

[20] Nein, nein, Salome; das ist es nicht, was du begehrst! Hör nicht auf die Stimme deiner Mutter. Sie gab dir immer [15] schlechten Rat. Achte nicht auf sie.

SALOME

I pay no heed to the voice of my [14b, 14a] mother. For by my own desire I want the head of Jokanaan upon a shining silver charger. Remember the oath you've taken, yes, Herod. Remember the oath you've taken, do not forget.

Ich achte nicht auf die Stimme meiner Mutter. Zu meiner eignen Lust will ich den Kopf des Jochanaan in einer Silberschüssel haben. Du hast einen Eid geschworen, Herodes. Du hast einen Eid geschworen, vergiss das nicht!

HEROD
(hastily)

I know, I know the solemn oath I've [5] taken, I know it well. And I have sworn by all my gods above me But I now must beg of you Salome, come, ask for something else of me. Come, ask for the half of all my royal realm, and that I will give you. But don't demand I beg of you what you have just now demanded.

Ich weiss, ich habe einen Eid geschworen. Ich weiss es wohl. Bei meinen Göttern habe ich geschworen. Aber ich beschwöre dich, Salome, verlange etwas andres von mir. Verlange die Hälfte meines Königreichs. Ich will sie dir geben. Aber verlange nicht von mir, was deine Lippen verlangten.

SALOME
(powerfully)

I demand from your hands the head of Jokanaan.

Ich verlange von dir den Kopf des Jochanaan.

HEROD

No, no, I do not wish to give it. [20] Nein, nein, ich will ihn dir nicht geben.

SALOME

Remember the oath you've taken, Herod.

Du hast einen Eid geschworen, Herodes.

HERODIAS

Yes, remember the oath you've taken. You have sworn before us all.

Ja, du hast einen Eid geschworen. Alle haben es gehört.

HEROD

Peace, woman, for I did not speak to you.

[20] Still, Weib, zu dir spreche ich nicht.

HERODIAS

My daughter does right when she demands the head of Jokanaan as her guerdon. He's brought such disgrace and shame on my head. It's quite clear she still loves her mother well. Do not yield, my daughter, do not yield! Remember the oath he's taken.

Meine Tochter hat recht daran getan, den Kopf des Jochanaan zu verlangen. Er hat mich mit Schimpf und Schande bedeckt. Man kann sehn, dass sie ihre [14b]Mutter liebt. Gib nicht nach, meine Tochter, gib nicht nach. Er hat einen Eid geschworen.

HEROD

Peace! I'll hear no more! Salome, I must

Still, sprich nicht zu mir! Salome, ich

49

beg of you. Don't be stubborn! Look, I've always felt so much love for you. Maybe my love for you was far too much. So do not ask me for this one thing. The head of a human, hacked from off his body, would be foul to look on. Mark what I tell you. I have an emerald stone. The finest emerald in all this world of ours. You'd like to own it perhaps? Then ask it of me, I'll give you this jewel, the finest of all.

[6, 16] beschwöre dich: Sei nicht trotzig! Sieh, ich habe dich immer lieb gehabt. Kann sein, ich habe dich zu lieb gehabt. Darum verlange das nicht von mir. Der Kopf eines Mannes, der vom Rumpf getrennt ist, ist ein übler Anblick. Hör', was ich sage! Ich habe einen Smaragd. Er ist der schönste Smaragd der ganzen Welt. Den willst du haben, nicht wahr? Verlang ihn von mir, ich will ihn dir geben, den schönsten Smaragd.

SALOME

I ask for the head of Jokanaan.

[14b]Ich fordre den Kopf des Jochanaan.

HEROD

But you're not listening. But you're not listening. Allow me to speak to you, Salome!

[14a, 20] Du hörst nicht zu, du hörst nicht zu. Lass mich zu dir reden, Salome!

SALOME

The head of Jokanaan.

[14b]Den Kopf des Jochanaan.

HEROD

You still say that just to torment me, all because I stared at your body. But your beauty made me confused. Oh! Oh! Bring wine! I'm thirsty. Salome, Salome, let us be friends with one another, now. Consider . . . Ah! What was I saying? Yes, what? Ah! Now I remember! Salome, you know of my snow-white peacocks, all my lovely, snow-white peacocks, as they strut around in the myrtle gardens. Now all of these, all, yes, all, I'll give you. There's no king alive, who has peacocks that can compare with these. I've barely a hundred. But I'd give you all these, with pleasure.

[14a]Das sagst du nur, um mich zu quälen, weil ich dich so angeschaut habe. Deine [5a, 20] Schönheit hat mich verwirrt. Oh! Oh! [21] Bringt Wein! Mich dürstet. Salome, Salome, lass uns wie Freunde, zu einander sein! Bedenk dich! Ah! Was [16] wollt ich sagen? Was war's? Ah! Ich weiss es wieder! Salome, du kennst meine weissen Pfauen, meine schönen, weissen Pfauen, die im Garten zwischen den Myrten wandeln. Ich will sie dir alle, alle geben. In der ganzen Welt lebt kein König, der solche Pfauen hat. Ich habe blos hundert. Aber alle will ich dir geben.

SALOME

Give me the head of Jokanaan!

Gib mir den Kopf des Jochanaan.

HERODIAS

Wisely said, my dear daughter!

[11a] Gut gesagt, meine Tochter!

HEROD

Silence! You're screeching like a bird of prey.

[22] Still, Weib! Du kreischest wie ein Raubvogel.

HERODIAS
(*to Herod*)

And you, you're ridiculous, you and your peacocks!

Und du, du bist lächerlich mit deinen Pfauen.

HEROD

How I hate that voice of yours. Silence, I say! Salome, just think what you're doing. People say of this man that God has sent him. And he's a holy man. The Almighty's finger has touched his face. You cannot wish that I should come to harm, Salome? Listen to me!

[6] Deine Stimme peinigt mich. Still, sag [21] ich dir! Salome, bedenk, was du tun willst. Es kann sein, dass der Mann von [4b] Gott gesandt ist. Er ist ein heil'ger Mann. Der Finger Gottes hat ihn [21] berührt. Du möchtest nicht, dass mich ein Unheil trifft, Salome? Hör' jetzt auf mich!

SALOME

I want the head of Jokanaan.

[14b]Ich will den Kopf den Jochanaan.

HEROD
(flaring up)

You will not even listen. Be calm, Salome. I am, you see, quite calm now.

[14a]Ah! Du willst nicht auf mich hören. Sei ruhig, Salome. Ich, siehst du, bin ruhig.

(low and secret)

Listen: I've secretly hidden away some jewels of mine. These jewels even your own mother's eyes have never seen. I'll show you a necklace with four bands of rubies, a topaz, yellow as the eye of a tiger. A lighted topaz, like the eye of a wood pigeon, a green coloured topaz, like mountain cat's eyes. I've sumptuous opals for ever burning with hidden fires, cold as ice. And all of these I will give you, yes, all.

Höre: Ich habe an diesem Ort Juwelen versteckt, Juwelen, die selbst deine Mutter nie gesehen hat. Ich habe ein Halsband mit vier Reihen Perlen, Topase, gelb wie die Augen der Tiger. Topase, hellrot wie die Augen der Waldtaube, und grüne Topase, wie Katzenaugen. Ich habe Opale, die immer funkeln, mit einem Feuer, kalt wie Eis. [20] Ich will sie dir alle geben, alle.

(with still more agitation)

I've chrysolites in plenty, chrysoberyls, [21] chrysoprases, pearls unnumbered. And I have onyx stones and hyacinth clusters and dusky red cornelians. I'll give to you all these jewels, all of these and many others. My crystal ball could be yours, the law forbids any woman to look in it. Inside a precious pearly casket I've secreted three most wonderful sapphires. Whoever wears them on his brow has power to see many hidden things. These are priceless, fabulous treasures. Say what else d'you wish for, Salome? All your secret desires I'll gladly grant you, yes, all save one. You may not ask me [20] for the life of this prophet. I'll give you the mantle the High Priest holds most sacred. I'll give you the curtains that veil the Holy of Holies . . .

Ich habe Chrysolithe und Berylle, Chrysoprase and Rubine. Ich habe Sardonyx und Hyacinthsteine und Steine von Chalcedon. Ich will sie dir alle geben, alle und noch andre Dinge. Ich habe einen Kristall, in den zu schaun keinem Weibe vergönnt ist. In einem Perlenmutterkästchen habe ich drei wunderbare Türkise: wer sie an seiner Stirne trägt, kann Dinge sehn, die nicht wirklich sind. Es sind unbezahlbare Schätze. Was begehrst du sonst noch, Salome? Alles, was du verlangst, will ich dir geben, nur eines nicht. Nur nicht das Leben dieses einen Mannes. Ich will dir den Mantel des Hohenpriesters geben. Ich will dir den Vorhang des Allerheiligsten geben.

JEWS

Oh! Oh! Oh!

Oh! Oh! Oh!

SALOME
(ferociously)

Give me the head of Jokanaan!

Gib mir den Kopf des Jochanaan!

Herod, in despair, sinks back in his seat.
[15, 16, 18]

HEROD
(faintly)

Let her be given what she desires! She is, for certain, her own mother's child.

[14b]Man soll ihr geben, was sie verlangt! Sie ist in Wahrheit ihrer Mutter Kind.

Herodias draws from the hand of the Tetrarch the ring of death and gives it to the First Soldier, who straightway bears it to the Executioner.
[14a, 11a]

Who has taken my ring away?

Wer hat meinen Ring genommen?

The Executioner goes down into the cistern.

I know there was a ring upon my hand, here. Who has drunk the wine they gave me? There was wine here in my goblet.

Ich hatte einen Ring an meiner rechten Hand. Wer hat meinen Wein getrunken? Es war Wein in meinem Becher. Er war

51

Yes, it was full of wine and one of you has dared to drink it. Oh! I'm sure misfortune lies in store for someone.

mit Wein gefüllt. Es hat ihn jemand ausgetrunken. Oh! Gewiss wird Unheil über einen kommen.

HERODIAS

My daughter has done what's right!

Meine Tochter hat recht getan!

HEROD

Yes, I'm certain fearful misfortune is near.

[4b] Ich bin sicher, es wird ein Unheil geschehn.

Salome leans over the cistern and listens.

SALOME

I hear no noise from below there. There's not a sound! Why does the man not call for help? Ah! If anyone came down to kill me, I know I'd struggle, I know I'd start shouting, I know I could not face it! Now strike, now strike, [14a, 1a] Naaman, now strike, I command . . . No, there's not a sound. What means this terrible silence? Ah! There's something fallen down on the paving. I'm sure that something's fallen. That was the sword of the headsman. He's afraid, is that [4b] Naaman. He's let his sword slip from his fingers! He's terrified to behead him. He's naught but a coward, is that headsman. Send the soldiers down!

Es ist kein Laut zu vernehmen. Ich höre nichts. Warum schreit er nicht, der Mann? Ah! Wenn einer mich zu töten käme, ich würde schreien, ich würde mich wehren, ich würde es nicht dulden! Schlag' zu, schlag' zu, Naaman, schlag' zu, sag' ich dir . . . Nein, ich höre nichts. Es ist eine schreckliche Stille! Ah! Es ist etwas zu Boden gefallen. Ich hörte etwas fallen. Es war das Schwert des Henkers. Er hat Angst, dieser Sklave. Er hat das Schwert fallen lassen! Er traut sich nicht, ihn zu töten. Er ist eine Memme, dieser Sklave. Schickt Soldaten hin!

(to the Page)

You, come here, were you the friend of the man who died there? Well then, you mark my words: there are not yet enough dead men. Tell the soldiers they must not delay, they must go down below there, and bring me quickly that which I long for, that which the Tetrarch promised, that which is [14b, 14a] my own now! You hear me, you soldiers, get down into the cistern, this moment, and bring me the head of the prisoner!

Komm hierher, du warst der Freund dieses Toten, nicht? Wohlan, ich sage dir: es sind noch nicht genug Tote. Geh zu den Soldaten und befiehl ihnen, hinabzusteigen und mir zu holen, was ich verlange, was der Tetrarch mir versprochen hat, was mein ist! Hierher, ihr Soldaten, geht ihr in die Cisterne hinunter und holt mir den Kopf des Mannes!

(shouting)

Tetrarch, Tetrarch, give orders to your soldiers, bid them bring the head of Jokanaan, quickly!

Tetrarch, Tetrarch, befiehl deinen Soldaten, dass sie mir den Kopf des Jochanaan holen!

A huge black arm of the executioner comes forth from the cistern, bearing on a silver shield the head of Jokanaan. Salome seizes it.

[1, 14a]

Ah! A while ago you would not let me kiss your mouth, Jokanaan! Well, now I will taste your kisses. These teeth [11, 8, 1] of mine are waiting to bite deeply, as hungry teeth desire to bite ripened fruit. Yes, for I will now kiss, kiss your [12] mouth Jokanaan. I said that I would. Is [10a] that not the truth? Yes, I said that I would. Ah! Ah! Yes, I will now kiss your [12] mouth . . . But why, but why do you not look at me, Jokanaan? And your eyes [8] that were so terrifying, so full of scorn [11] and resentment, are now unseeing. Why are they so unseeing? Lift those heavy eyelids and let your eyes be opened, [1a]

Ah! Du wolltest mich nicht deinen Mund küssen lassen, Jochanaan! Wohl, ich werde ihn jetzt küssen! Ich will mit meinen Zähnen hineinbeissen, wie man in eine reife Frucht beisen mag. Ja, ich will ihn jetzt küssen, deinen Mund, Jochanaan. Ich hab' es gesagt. Hab' ich's nicht gesagt? Ja, ich hab' es gesagt. Ah! Ah! Ich will ihn jetzt küssen . . . Aber warum siehst du mich nicht an, Jochanaan? Deine Augen, die so schreckliche waren so voller Wut und Verachtung, sind jetzt geschlossen? Warum sind sie geschlossen? Offne doch die Augen, erhebe deine Lider,

Jokanaan! But why do you not look at me? Do I frighten you, Jokanaan, that you will not look at me now? Your tongue is silent, your tongue is mute, [19] Jokanaan. Yes, that scarlet viper which [1a] spat its venom here at my feet! It is curious, no? How comes it, that this poor, scarlet viper now stirs no more? You said many evil things of me, yes, of [8] me, Salome, the daughter of Herodias, and Princess of Judæa. Well then! I'm still alive, but you are dead, and your [4b] head, your head belongs to me! It's mine to do with as I wish. I may have it given to feed watch-dogs, or the birds of the air. What the dogs may leave [5a, 1a, 14a] behind them, will be devoured by the starving vultures. Ah! Ah! Jokanaan, [11] Jokanaan, you were fair. Your body was an ivory column with feet made of silver. It was a garden full of songbirds where the silver lilies gleamed. Naught [9] in this world was so white as your flesh. Naught in this world was as black as your hair. In this world of ours was naught so red as your mouth. Then your voice was like a sweet, scented vase, and [10a] when I looked on you I could hear mysterious, magical tones. [8]

Jochanaan! Warum siehst du mich nicht an? Hast du Angst vor mir, Jochanaan, dass du mich nicht an sehen willst? Und deine Zunge, sie spricht kein Wort, Jochanaan, diese Scharlachnatter, die ihren Geifer gegen mich spie. Es ist seltsam, nicht? Wie kommt es, dass diese rote Natter sich nicht mehr rührt? Du sprachst böse Worte gegen mich, gegen mich, Salome, die Tochter der Herodias, Prinzessin von Judäa. Nun wohl! Ich lebe noch, aber du bist tot, und dein Kopf, dein Kopf gehört mir. Ich kann mit ihm tun, was ich will. Ich kann ihn den Hunden vorwerfen, und den Vögeln der Luft. Was die Hunde übrig lassen, sollen die Vögel der Luft verzehren ... Ah! Ah! Jochanaan, Jochanaan, du warst schön. Dein Leib war ein Elfenbeinsäule auf silbernen Füssen. Er war ein Garten voller Tauben in der Silberlilien Glanz. Nichts in der Welt war so weiss wie dein Leib. Nichts in der Welt war so schwarz wie dein Haar. In der ganzen Welt war nichts so rot wie dein Mund. Deine Stimme war ein Weirauchgefäss, und wenn ich dich ansah hörte ich geheimnisvolle, Musik ...

She is lost in thought as she gazes upon Jokanaan's head.

Ah! And why did you never look at me, Jokanaan? Your eyes were veiled and all [5a] unheeding, like one who laboured to see his God shining in glory. Well! Maybe [4b] you have seen your God, Jokanaan, but me, me, me, you have never seen. If you [4c] had looked at me, you'd have loved me, [12] I know! I'm thrusting to taste your beauty. I hunger to taste your flesh. No wine nor fruit cold banish all my fevered yearning... What shall I do now, Jokanaan? All the rivers, all the surging waters cannot quench the fire of my desire and longing... Oh! But why did [11] you not look at me? If you'd but once looked at me you would have given your love. I know for sure you would [8, 1a, 9] have given your love. The glorious secret of love is mightier than is the secret of death.

Ah! Warum hast du mich nicht angesehn, Jochanaan? Du legtest über deine Augen die Binde eines, der seinen Gott schauen wollte. Wohl, du hast deinen Gott gesehn, Jochanaan, aber mich, mich, mich hast du nie gesehn. Hättest du mich gesehn, du hättest mich geliebt! Ich dürste nach deiner Schönheit. Ich hungre nach deinem Leib. Nicht Wein noch Äpfel können mein Verlangen stillen ... Was soll ich jetzt tun, Jochanaan? Nicht die Fluten, noch die grossen Wasser können dieses brünstige Begehren löschen ... Oh! Warum sahst du mich nicht an? Hättest du mich angesehn du hättest mich geliebt. Ich weiss es wohl, du hättest mich geliebt. Und das Geheimnis der Liebe ist grösser als das Geheimnis des Todes ...

HEROD
(with lowered voice, to Herodias)

You have an evil monster for a daughter. [11a] You mark my words, she is an evil [16] monster.

Sie ist ein Ungeheuer, deine Tochter. Ich sage dir, sie ist ein Ungeheuer!

HERODIAS
(forcefully)

My daughter has rightly judged. I wish to stay here with her.

Meine Tochter hat recht getan. Ich möchte jetzt hier bleiben.

HEROD

Ah! There speaks my own brother's wife.

Ah! Da spricht meines Bruders Wei?

53

Come, I'll not stay out here a moment longer.

(weaker)

[1a, 18] Komm, ich will nicht an diesen Orte bleiben.

(vehemently)

Come, come, I say! Surely some disaster is at hand. We'll hide away there inside the Palace. Herodias, my hands are starting to tremble.

[11a] Komm, sag' ich dir! Sicher, es wird Schreckliches geschehn. Wir wollen uns im Palast vergergen, Herodias, ich fange [16] an zu erzittern...

The moon disappears. Herod jumps up.

Mannasseh, Isachar, Ozias put the torches out. Come, veil the moon, come, veil the starlight!

Manasseh, Isachar, Ozias, löscht die Fackeln aus. Verbergt den Mond, verbergt die Sterne!

It becomes very dark.

For some disaster is at hand.

[16] Es wird Schreckliches geschehn.

SALOME
(faintly)

Ah! Now I have kissed your mouth at last, Jokanaan. Ah! Ah yes, I have at last kissed your mouth. There was a bitter lingering taste upon your lips. Could it be blood I taste? No! For it may be the taste of love... They tell me that the taste of love is bitter... But what of that? What of that? For I have kissed your mouth at last Jokanaan. Yes, now I have kissed, kissed your mouth.

[11a] Ah! Ich habe deinen Mund geküsst, Jochanaan. Ah! Ich habe ihn geküsst, deinen Mund, was war ein bitterer Geschmack auf deinen Lippen. Hat es nach Blut geschmeckt? Nein! Doch es [12] schmeckte vielleicht nach Liebe... Sie sagen, dass die Liebe bitter schmecke... [9, 11a, 1a] Allein was tut's? Was tut's? Ich habe deinen Mund geküsst, Jochanaan. Ich [10a] habe ihn geküsst, deinen Mund.

[9]

The moon breaks through again and illuminates Salome.

HEROD
(turning round)

Go, crush that girl to death!

Man töte dieses Weib!

[14a]

The soldiers rush forward and crush Salome under their shields.

[22, 1a]

The curtain falls quickly.

Stephanie Sundine as Salome in André Engel's production for Welsh National Opera (photo: Zoë Dominic)

Hofmannsthal's 'Elektra': from drama to libretto

Kenneth Segar

'A drama freely based on Sophocles' is Hofmannsthal's sub-title for his *Elektra* of 1903, and this simple statement not only indicates the subject-matter of his play but also alludes to a major problem he was facing. Turning to Sophocles betokened Hofmannsthal's desire to keep faith with the rich substance of past culture; but he had increasingly learned that this was something which could also be burdensome and debilitating. Knowing several languages, at home not only in German literature but in that of ancient Greece and Rome, of Italy, of the Spanish baroque, of France and England, he had found himself a poet capable of creating aesthetic harmonies out of the fusion of his own intensely experienced present and the heritage of an age-old world. All his experience was, in fact, filtered through the themes and forms of millenia of pagan and Judaeo–Christian art, and the result was that self, past and present came to exist as a harmonious totality. His state of mind was, he claimed, quasi-mystical or 'magical', one in which every facet of life seemed to cohere; everything was 'equally near, equally distant', sometimes as though he were 'at the centre of a perfect sphere'. This richness of transmitted culture could, however, also create a sense of living outside of time that was less than happy: Hofmannsthal remarks that he often felt as though he lived only in pre-cast moulds, in mere ritual repetitions of the thoughts and acts 'of the last three thousand years'. 'We cannot open our mouths,' he had written on behalf of his aestheticising generation, 'without ten thousand dead people speaking through us.' He is like 'a ghost wandering in broad daylight, thinking others' thoughts, feeling others' feelings, the world appearing as though behind a veil'. Experienced thus, the past robs one of a sense of living in the real world. So, 'pre-existence', the term Hofmannsthal used for this whole mode of relating to reality, had both wondrously positive ('magical') qualities, but also potentially disastrous ones. Around the turn of the century, as the adolescent poet was reaching adulthood, this latter sense of the unreality of life reached crisis proportions. Hofmannsthal expressed the crisis in a famous prose-narrative, 'Ein Brief' ('A Letter') of 1902. Here, Philip Lord Chandos, a man of letters, tells of the terrible malaise from which he is suffering. He has lost all sense of reality: that positive inter-connectedness of all things has turned into its negative obverse, namely that nothing has greater substance than anything else, that the world has thereby become for him a ghostly charade, and that he is now, with respect to the simplest utterances and actions, in a state of paralysis.

Hofmannsthal's *Elektra* drama stands very close to this crisis. The play is in many ways a discussion of it in terms of the individual's relationship to time and action, of the ability to live in a real present. This is clear from the treatment of the three major figures. Elektra is obsessed with the past in the form of her dead father, Agamemnon. She is so consumed by the presence of his shade that she can do nothing but engage in constant, ritual conjuration of his murder at the hands of her mother, Klytemnestra, and her mother's paramour, Aegisthus; she can only indulge in fond imagining of the vengeance that will one day be exacted and of the triumphant dance that she and her returning brother, Orestes, will perform on the murderers' graves. But those who feed so obsessively off the past, and the imaginings which stem from it, lose their power to act in the real world. When Orestes does indeed return, and the time comes for her to hand over the buried axe, her instrument of retribution, she simply forgets to perform the act so often rehearsed in imagination. Twice she laments: 'I could not even give him the axe!' So imprisoned is she in sterile imaginings that she can scarcely find the strength even to begin the triumphant dance on which she has brooded for so long. Psychoanalytic interpreters (Heinz Politzer, Ritchie Robertson) have shown how Elektra's problem is one of hysteria associated with her father-fixation. And it does, indeed, appear that Hofmannsthal has projected his aesthetic problem onto a contemporary concern with sexual hysteria. We know that he had recently read the *Studies on Hysteria* by Freud and Breuer; that he knew the sexual explanation of Hamlet's behaviour to be found in Freud's *Interpretation of Dreams* — he later referred to Elektra as a Hamlet-figure; and that he had read Hermann Bahr's psychoanalytic view of Greek tragedy. There is a wealth of sexual allusion in the language and behaviour of Elektra: she cries out to her dead father against his 'wife and the one who sleeps with her in one bed, in your royal bed'; there is crude voyeuristic imagery, perversion of natural feeling — the axe as the child born of her father-fixation —, even the dance seen as the 'trance-like state' experienced by some hysterics. There is certainly enough evidence to claim that Elektra is a powerful portrayal of neurotic failure.

Klytemnestra is also imprisoned in sterility, her relationship to the present as flawed as Elektra's own, but for the diametrically opposite reason. Whereas Elektra will not let go of her past, Klytemnestra is desperate for the past not to have been, for no criminal act to have occurred. 'Ourselves and deeds. What sort of language is that? [. . .] There was a Before, then an After — but there was no deed.' This denial of her past action turns out to be no solution to the problem of the past, but equally deprives her of a present lived reality: now Klytemnestra hates Elektra, now needs and wants her, now shrinks from her in fear, now triumphs over her; she has helped to murder Agamemnon, but if he returned (she assures the amazed Elektra) she would talk with him as with an old friend. There is no stay in this fluid, impressionistic mind. Klytemnestra's repressed past haunts her in the form of bad dreams, creates terrors about a future to be warded off with a weight of talismans, leaves her present merely an escapist flux. Nor does the third figure, Chrysothemis, elude the atmosphere of hysterical fixation on the past. Her desire to give herself to life, love, marriage, children, remains thwarted by her enforced presence in this claustrophobic, haunted palace. Her reality is bounded by a frustrated sexuality, as normal as Elektra's appears perverted: 'I want a woman's destiny', she pleads with the relentless Elektra, but she is not shown requited, and all we see is a Chrysothemis whose reality is also blurred, 'disordered'. She needs a god to give her an 'inner light so that she can find herself again'.

So has Hofmannsthal created, out of his aesthetic crisis rooted in an unhealthy relationship to the past, a rather typical 'fin-de-siècle' work of hysterical fixation, obsession, frustration? On the one hand, clearly he has, but we must recall the ambivalence in Hofmannsthal's attitude to the past: it was both destructive and sacred. From the latter perspective, may we not view Elektra herself as also embodying a positive meaning? Although she has been reduced to the level of an animal living off scraps in the palace-yard, and is frequently described (even by herself) as an animal, she does fervently

THE OPERA THAT WILL "ELEKTRIFY" LONDON.

TO SING THE MOST ARDUOUS SCORE EVER WRITTEN: CHARACTERS IN STRAUSS'S "ELEKTRA,"
TO BE PRODUCED FOR THE FIRST TIME AT COVENT GARDEN ON SATURDAY.

The London première of 'Elektra' in 1910: Friedrich Weidemann as Orestes, Edyth Walker as Elektra and Anna Bahr-Mildenburg as Klytemnestra (Royal Opera House Archives)

proclaim: 'I am not an animal. *I cannot forget!*' Compared to this, Klytemnestra's desire to deny the past is immoral; and Chrysothemis' longed-for 'destiny', it is made clear to us, is tainted with Klytemnestra's desire to forget: 'Daughter of my mother!' Elektra taunts, alluding to her sister's collusion with the murderers to wipe out all memory of Agamemnon. Are we surprised that Hofmannsthal's stage-directions portray Klytemnestra as utterly decayed, dragging herself painfully on her stick, supported by her minion, grotesquely painted and bejewelled to give a semblance of life? And, in her confrontations with the intensely suffering Elektra, surely Chrysothemis — the one who seems cut out for a healthy relationship to time and action — appears shallow and banal. Does not Hofmannsthal want us to feel Elektra's moral superiority as she jealously guards the sacred memory of her betrayed father, keeping faith with her past? In fact, there is evidence in the text of Hofmannsthal's desire to write a heroic tragedy. At the close, Elektra passes beyond all confrontation, all words, to dance 'with every fibre of her being her dance of triumph'. She is described in the stage-directions as 'throwing back her head like a Maenad, thrusting her knees high in forward movement, flinging her arms wide apart: it is a dance of indescribable intensity.' The reference is to the wild dance of the Bacchantes, followers of the god Dionysos, performing their ecstatic celebration of the grandeur of life in all its destructive power. This is no longer Freud or Hermann Bahr, but Nietzsche's *Birth of Tragedy*: against the screams of the sacrificial victims (Klytemnestra, Aegisthus and their entourage) Elektra triumphantly asserts her fidelity to the dead Agamemnon as an expression of her oneness with the order of things. In dancing and dying, Elektra is both regaining the true self that she has had taken from her and is re-entering the ground of Being, a state in which she feels a heavy but visionary joy.

Strangely, neither the neurotic nor Dionysian perspective leaves us with a sense of drama. Elektra's death, whether neurotic failure or triumphant regaining of her true self, is merely the ultimate intensification of her condition. But this had not been Hofmannsthal's intention in writing the *Elektra* drama. He had gone back to the ancient Greek dramatist in order to learn how to overcome the 'indecent' narcissism of the lyric voice and write for the 'real, brutal stage' with its dialectic of conflict and resolution. Our analysis suggests how far he is from the dramatic conflict of his Greek model. Sophocles had, admittedly, emphasised the psychological problems (including the sexual) emanating from larger, public concerns — morality, legitimacy, the re-establishment of order — but these personal reactions still relate to the larger issues and still create external conflict and drama. Hofmannsthal has, however, so completely internalised the problems of his characters that there is no actual conflict left. His distance from the public concerns of his predecessor (and the creation of a drama of conflict out of them) is apparent in his highlighting a *solitary* Elektra. And this is also true of his handling of the murdered Agamemnon: Klytemnestra is not made to justify her act by reference to Agamemnon's sacrifice of their daughter Iphigenia at Aulis. Equally, the public importance of Orestes' retributive deed recedes to the margins of the work. After the Berlin première of the play, the critic Maximilian Harden commented that there would have been greater coherence without Orestes' deed; and in privately admitting the rightness of this judgment, Hofmannsthal was essentially denying that the work is one of conflict and dramatic shape. He confessed, in 1911, that he had ended up turning Sophocles' drama into a 'vehicle for emotion', presumably referring to the fact that we are given only a range of intensely lived situations. First, there are the emotional predicaments of the three women — Elektra living with her fixation and in an agony of suspense, Klytemnestra in fear, Chrysothemis in frustration; then, there are the powerful feelings of the recognition scene between brother and sister; finally, we experience Elektra's joy and the wild dance of triumph. Clearly, we are back with a lyric voice. Whether the subject-matter is hysteria or mystic union with the ground of Being, the work is less a drama than a tone-poem.

* * *

A tone-poem lacking music forced Hofmannsthal to use every other possible means to intensify his utterance. To begin with, the language of the play is essentially not communicative; rather, words are stretched to their *expressive* limits. The three women are imprisoned in their respective fixation, fear, frustration, and merely express the intensity of their personal, uncomprehended feeling, for words cannot bridge the gulf between speaker and interlocutor. Elektra knows, too, that her true self cannot be expressed except by 'dancing and remaining silent'. This strange inadequacy of words reflects a second problem of Hofmannsthal's: the Chandos 'Letter' reveals not only an impaired relationship to reality, but — more baleful still for a writer — that the very power of words to communicate reality has become suspect. Words are like 'rotting mushrooms' in Chandos' mouth. Hofmannsthal, alluding to a

Ernestine Schumann-Heink as Klytemnestra and Annie Krull as Elektra in the Dresden première, 1909 (Royal Opera House Archives)

well-documented general crisis of language at the turn of the century, wrote that his whole generation 'had seen through words'. Among writers this scepticism about the efficacy of language took the form of an overwhelming desire to experiment with the non-verbal arts: mime, pantomime, ballet (in 1900, Hofmannsthal had asked Strauss to compose music for a ballet he had written, but Strauss had declined) and modern dance — Elektra's (like Salome's) is in keeping with contemporary fascination with the dancer Isadora Duncan. So, in his *Elektra*, Hofmannsthal plays up every non-verbal means of creating mood and atmosphere. His stage-directions and long production-note of 1903 make clear how important he considered *décor* (the claustrophobic courtyard, which he later drew for Strauss), *lighting* (blood-red patches in the gloom, the use of torches), *costume* (Elektra's rags, Klytemnestra's blood-red dress), *acoustic effects* (the overseer's whiplash, the deathly silence preceding Orestes' entry into the palace, the climax beyond words), and finally *gesture* (Elektra frenziedly digging for the axe, ominously circling round Aegisthus with her torch, dancing exultantly).

But Hofmannsthal always thought that the best medium for the creation of atmosphere, mood, intensity, even a 'higher reality', was music. Chandos, at the close of the 'Letter', writes hopefully of one day working in 'a material more immediate, more fluid, glowing more intensely than words'. And when Strauss approached Hofmannsthal about using his *Elektra* as a libretto, the poet jumped at the chance of music, which would present his vision 'more powerfully than any poetry could'. On the other hand, the composer, who needed a verbal and visual programme, can only have been struck by the expressive qualities of the drama as we have outlined them. And it must have been even more enticing to find that the work is made up of seven clearly defined sections, inviting (as Norman Del Mar has shown) the kind of symphonic structuring that the composer had used in his tone-poems and *Salome*: the work begins with the maidservants and overseer, moves into Elektra's great opening monologue, then brings Elektra together with Chrysothemis, Elektra with Klytemnestra, Elektra again with Chrysothemis, Elektra with Orestes, and culminates in the great coda where all are 'symphonically' present — Elektra celebrating the deaths of Klytemnestra and Aegisthus at the hands of Orestes, Chrysothemis joyful at the thought of release, the shade of Agamemnon towering over the scene. Thus, the collaboration of poet and musician is to their mutual advantage. Hofmannsthal can give his poetic work ultimate intensity, and Strauss can find his musical way forward. At no other moment is their working relationship so unproblematic: Strauss calls Hofmannsthal a 'born librettist', and the poet is delighted.

Yet Hofmannsthal's delight may also stem from two further advantages to be gained from re-working his text. By 1906 he is more distant from the 'Chandos crisis', and he takes the opportunity (whilst shortening passages and adding material as required by Strauss) firstly to emphasise the positive aspect of his heroine, and secondly to re-think his relationship to drama.

Hofmannsthal is quite aware that the composer of *Salome* can intensify the atmosphere of sexual hysteria and blood-lust. Interestingly, his earliest comments to Strauss attempt to distance his work from that opera — partly because Strauss is worried that he may be repeating himself and so is suggesting different subjects in place of *Elektra*, but partly because Hofmannsthal is himself concerned that the neurotic protagonist shall also be more palpably an heroic protagonist. He tells Strauss at the outset that he can

Pauline Tinsley as Elektra with Welsh National Opera in the Netherlands Opera production by Harry Kupfer, designed by Wilfried Werz (photo: Julian Sheppard)

already hear the future sequence of motifs 'surging upwards towards the victorious, purifying deed of Orestes'. No longer marginal, it is action and not paralysis that is to be the underlying sense of the opera. This added emphasis will, in turn, underscore Elektra's fidelity to the memory of her father, and so more powerfully evoke her tragic status. To this end, Hofmannsthal is happy to make important additions to the text of the drama. One addition ('Orest, Orest, Orest . . .') helps Strauss to create out of the recognition scene between brother and sister an ethereal moment of tenderness and rapt joy. Furthermore, Hofmannsthal gives Elektra a new final utterance, taken (via Erwin Rohde's *Psyche*) from a Persian mystic: 'Ah, love kills, but none passes through life without knowing love'. Her use of 'love' is in blatant contrast to the word 'love' uttered at the same moment by Chrysothemis, who is thinking of marriage and children. Elektra is thinking of the sacred memory of Agamemnon, and her path to that self-recovery which is also self-loss, since she thereby re-enters the ground of Being. We are meant to hear, in Hofmannsthal's words, the 'heroic voice against the humane voice', a point nicely made by Strauss's provision here of a warm melodic line for Chrysothemis against which Elektra pits her steely heroic declamation. Ritchie Robertson thinks Hofmannsthal guilty in the drama of 'a sentimental attempt to supply an up-beat ending which is incompatible with the sombre and violent events which have preceded it'. Clearly, in the opera, much depends upon the listener's response to Strauss's climactic music: does he conjure the fulfilment of that vision of ecstatic triumph expressed by Elektra in her great opening monologue? And, here, you may agree or disagree with

61

Heinz Politzer that the composer of the Dance of the Seven Veils does not achieve what the composer of *The Rite of Spring* could have!

And so to our final point: Hofmannsthal's re-thinking, through his work on the libretto, of his relationship to drama. He had wanted to write genuine drama of conflict and resolution, but he has begun to see that this is not his true style. His conservative mentality always seeks harmonies, not disruptions and radical resolutions. Strauss's leitmotivic and symphonic mode not only builds the musical structure to take us from Elektra's vision of retribution to the great coda, but also creates musical equivalents of what Hofmannsthal metaphorically calls 'configurations': the poet frequently uses this term for the relationships between characters grouped together on stage, referring to a 'contrapuntal' fusion of disparates, or the 'harmonising' of contradictory voices in ironic incomprehension. But he does not mean only the voices of his characters. He means, too, the contradictory voices within himself — decadent, humane, heroic. He means the conflation of personal problems and contemporary issues, positive and negative poles, tragedy and psycho-pathology, ancient and modern. From his intended depiction of life as conflict, Hofmannsthal has found his way back to wholeness and harmony. And this is because he can, by using the public stage and musical performance, ritualise, mythicise and so generalise what had been the 'indecent' narcissism of 'pre-existence'. In his late essay on *The Egyptian Helen* (1928), he reveals not only that this essentially lyric mode is his true voice, but also that he believes it to be the only appropriate way of writing for his refined and sophisticated age:

> How else can we capture our own present, engulfed as it is in thousands of years of culture — a culture which floods our very being with East and West, which creates such a range of awareness, such tension of contraries within this awareness, such a sense of Here yet Else-where? . . . No middle-class, everyday dialogue can capture this! Let us write mythological operas, the truest of all art forms, believe me!

Myth here means for Hofmannsthal the ceremonial enactment of the complexity of modern awareness, and opera is to ensure that this enactment attains its most heightened expression. This must be what he glimpsed right at the start with his *Elektra* collaboration. The way was already open for *Ariadne on Naxos*, *The Woman without a Shadow*, *The Egyptian Helen*, but equally for that mythicisation of Vienna 1740 — 'a half real, half imaginary wholeness' —, which is the subject of Hofmannsthal's second collaboration with Strauss, *Der Rosenkavalier*.

The following material (by writers named in my text) is of particular interest:
(1) Norman Del Mar, *Richard Strauss: a critical commentary on his life and works*, Vol. 1, 1962, pp. 287-333.
(2) Heinz Politzer, 'Hugo von Hofmannsthals "Elektra": Geburt der Tragödie aus dem Geiste der Psychopathologie', *Deutsche Vierteljahrsschrift für Literaturwissenschaft und Geistesgeschichte*, 47 (1973), pp. 95-119.
(3) Ritchie Robertson, '"Ich habe ihm das Beil nicht geben können": the Heroine's Failure in Hofmannsthal's "Elektra"', *Orbis Litterarum*, 41 (1986), pp. 312-331.

Elektra and the 'Elektra Complex'

Christopher Wintle

The circumstances surrounding the composition of *Elektra* are well enough known. As the first venture to come to fruition between the internationally established Richard Strauss (b. 1864) and the far less celebrated, but brilliant, Hugo von Hofmannsthal (b. 1874), it offered an even more luridly decadent portrait of a possessed heroine than had been the case with Strauss's immediately preceding *Salome* (1905), a work to which it bears obvious similarities. Although Hofmannsthal had adapted Sophocles' play by 1903, it was not until June 1906 that Strauss began to compose the music, drawing as he did so upon the wealth of experience he had gained in writing symphonic poems (*Elektra* was his opus 58). This experience was especially evident in the handling of the orchestra, which benefited from lavish divisions of the wind and brass parts, and in the large-scale control of musical contrasts. Described as a 'tragedy', the work unfolded in one extended act, creating thereby an especially taxing leading role, and was first performed on January 25, 1909. The impact was one of such overwhelming violence that it seemed neither desirable nor perhaps even possible to pursue its particular vein any further, and in subsequent works Strauss relaxed his style, and chose different kinds of subject matter.

Yet there are still things to be learnt from the fascination the work exerted around the time of its first appearance. In a critique of *Freud and Psychoanalysis* published in 1912, Jung advanced the idea of an 'Elektra complex', which explored a special sort of relationship between daughter and father. This was intended as a counterpart to Freud's 'Oedipus complex', which deals with the quasi-incestuous bond between son and mother. Whether by chance or not, Jung's complex offers an extraordinary parallel to aspects of Hofmannsthal's libretto, and just how this parallel works will be the subject of this essay. (Freud himself found Jung's idea interesting, though not strictly necessary. Like later analysts, he considered the Oedipus complex to cover daughters and fathers as well as sons and mothers.)

There is another way in which this opera caught the attention of contemporaries. As is well known, the Vienna School kept their eyes firmly fixed on Strauss's development in the early years of this century (later they turned them on Mahler). Egon Wellesz, a student friend of Berg and Webern, used to tell how he arrived one day for a composition lesson with Schoenberg, to find his teacher pouring over a score of *Salome*. How, he was wondering, could such innovations ever be surpassed? Yet, if anything, *Elektra* is even more musically innovative than *Salome*, and in certain respects its harmonic treatment exceeded in daring some of the most advanced progressions Schoenberg was to include in his harmony book (the *Harmonielehre*) published in 1911. In the final part of this essay, it will be shown how a few of these innovations grew directly out of the psychological issues of the work.

The 'Jungian' dimension to Hofmannsthal's thought begins to emerge as soon as the main alterations he made to Sophocles' play are placed under some interpretative scrutiny. Unlike the Greeks, Hofmannsthal was not concerned to assess the moral worth of his characters' actions, to discriminate between the good and the bad, or the right and the wrong in each instance. He was more concerned to explore and develop the tensions within a relatively closed family circle, in which the hysteria of one member, Elektra, holds all the others to ransom. This family comprises two sisters and a brother (Elektra, Chrysothemis and Orestes), their mother (Klytemnestra), and their mother's lover, Aegisthus. Many years before the start of the opera, their father, Agamemnon, has been murdered on his return from Troy by Klytemnestra and Aegisthus. Fearing reprisal, Klytemnestra banished Orestes, who ever since has lived far away from home. Elektra's hysteria arises from her fidelity to the memory of her murdered father; her sole sustaining hope is that Orestes will return to avenge the terrible deed by taking the lives of Klytemnestra and Aegisthus. Hofmannsthal enhances the portrait of her hysteria in three ways: by omitting Sophocles' chorus that argues, reasons and consoles; by avoiding any discussion between Elektra and her mother of the reasons for which Klytemnestra murdered Agamemnon; and finally, once Orestes has returned and taken revenge, by making Elektra die of her extreme nervous condition. (According to the Greeks — Aeschylus and Euripides, as well as Sophocles — she recovers and lives.)

The tensions within this family circle are revealed in the series of confrontations which forms the main body of the work. As Norman Del Mar points out, there are seven main sections, all but the first involving Elektra:

(1) the Maidservants;
(2) Elektra alone;
(3) Elektra and Chrysothemis;
(4) Elektra and Klytemnestra: this is followed by a rapid series of events precipitated by the false news of Orestes' death;
(5) Elektra and Chrysothemis again;
(6) Elektra and Orestes (who arrives at this point);
(7) the Dénouement, including the murders of Klytemnestra and Aegisthus, and Elektra's dance of death.

These sections dwell predominantly on the mental anguish suffered by the three main female characters, anguish that is corroborated by the physical condition to which each has been reduced.

In this discussion, the references to the ideas listed in the thematic guide are essentially to leitmotifs, the short, onomatopoeic musical figures that accumulate and discharge associations as the work unfolds, very much in the manner that Wagner devised. For the most part, the vocal lines are derived from the melodic and harmonic argument sustained in the orchestra. Occasionally there are more conventional aria or song-like passages: when these occur, they are used with some special significance. A discussion of form, tonality and harmony, however, is reserved almost entirely for the final part of the essay.

1. The Maidservants

The opera is set in the inner courtyard of the palace at Mycenae. In this introductory section, five maidservants and their overseer describe Elektra's behaviour, and strongly dispute her merits. There is no overture as such, merely a statement of a four-bar motif which establishes the commanding psychological presence in the community of the murdered Agamemnon [1a]. Strauss transforms this motif to accompany the various descriptions of Elektra's appearance, thereby relating the psychological to the physical from

learn

The Maids and the Overseer in the Netherlands Opera production, 1977 (photo: Jaap Pieper)

the outset. She is reputed, for example, to lie on the ground groaning [1b] and howling [1c] for her father. Throughout the opera there are many such transformations. Essential too to the musical tapestry is the abundance of illustrative (onomatopeic) figures. (There are so many that only a handful can be included in the thematic guide.) Their function is to sustain the relentlessly taut nervous atmosphere. For example, motif [2a] describes Elektra's poisonous 'wild-cat' glances, establishing the bestial imagery of the opera; motif [2b] her attempts to strike her servants; motif [2c] the sympathy of one of the maids who reminds the others of Elektra's royal descent [4b and 5]; and motif [2d], the flagellation of this maid by the others, the first instance where a threat leads to punishment. Elektra herself is momentarily glimpsed, springing back 'like a wild animal' [3]. She is reported to have excoriated the maidservants for their sexual indulgence, an accusation that significantly relates, as we shall see, to her own sexual difficulties.

2. Elektra alone
The 'Jungian' elements now come to the fore. Elektra enters, and finds herself alone; she is profoundly conscious of her own unresolved tensions [4a], and openly laments her lost father [5]. It is known that hysterics can preserve

65

traumatic memories vividly intact for an indefinite period, with a propensity for these memories to reactivate themselves through associations of time and place. (In 1893, Freud and Breuer wrote: 'ideas which have become pathological have persisted with such freshness and affective strength because they have been denied the normal wearing-away processes by means of abreaction and reproduction in states of uninhibited association.') That it is the anniversary of the murder by Klytemnestra [6] and Aegisthus [7] of Agamemnon in his bath inspires Elektra to relive the trauma in ghastly detail. Here Strauss's music potently illustrates the steam from the bathwater and the flowing of blood [8a]. (One might usefully compare Sieglinde's trauma at the end of Act Two of *The Valkyrie*.) Two important motifs emerge: the first represents the inexorable demand for retribution that seems to emanate from Agamemnon [9], and the second tenderly invokes Elektra's childhood, and what Melanie Klein would have called the good (as opposed to the bad) family she once knew [10].

At this central point in her soliloquy, Elektra refers to herself as Agamemnon's 'Kind', his child. Yet she is a mature woman, and it is only circumstances that have prevented her from growing away from her father, from making what Jung described as an 'unconscious fantasy of sacrifice symbolic of the giving up of infantile wishes' (as one example of such a sacrifice he cited Siegfried's slaughtering of the dragon, a mother archetype). This restraint has profound consequences for her sexuality but one of its direct consequences is that she 'displays violent resistances' against her mother, while adopting 'a particularly affectionate and dependent' attitude to her dead father. Unless resolved, Jung warned, such 'violent resistances' can 'lead to murder'.

Elektra then reveals, with an intense *Schadenfreude*, precisely these murderous impulses. Her vision of the rivers of blood that would flow in retribution are matched by even more extravagant illustrative music (the horses and hounds must also die), laced with grimly threatening versions of the Agamemnon motif [1b], and a portentous destiny figure [8b]. This vision culminates in a grotesque, imaginary dance of victory [11], shot through with vindicating references to the good family [10], and concluding with a triumphal reiteration of Agamemnon's name [1d].

3. Elektra and Chrysothemis

Ironically, Elektra's attitude is thrown into dramatic relief by the complete contrast offered in the work's third section, inaugurated by the interruption of her sister, Chrysothemis, who calls soothingly to her (the motif, [30], is developed much later). The startled Elektra reminds Chrysothemis [12] of the axe that felled their father [13] before proceeding to vilify her as her 'mother's daughter' [14a and b]. The charge is less than fair. Chrysothemis has come to warn her sister of the plan [15] to incarcerate her in a dark tower. Laughing contemptuously, Elektra urges that instead all the palace doors be locked [8c], and that Chrysothemis should join her at the gates, praying for the Day of Judgement. Chrysothemis' extended, vehement refusal to do this comprises the main body of this section, and is cast as a stable, monolithic musical structure of a basically lyrical kind, in triple time. It conveys the anxiety that drives her through the palace [16a], caught in the fear which Elektra [4a] has generated through her preoccupation with Agamemnon [5]. Indeed, it is because of Elektra that she has been forbidden to bear children (in Klytemnestra's eyes, potential avengers), which she longs to do [16b] just as

Rose Pauly as Elektra with Hilde Konetzni as Chrysothemis at Covent Garden in 1938 (Royal Opera House Archives)

her friends have already done, before it is too late [16c]. For her, Agamemnon, however sadly, is dead and gone, Orestes unlikely to return; the frustration of her sexual energy and maternal instincts seems pointless. The insistence of the climactic music, however, underlines the futility of arguing with Elektra, and she dissolves into tears [12].

At this point, both sisters become aware of the approach of their mother. Chrysothemis flees, but not before divulging that Klytemnestra has had a terrible dream [18] causing her to shriek out in the night (in this anxiety nightmare, Orestes is pursuing her) [19]. Fortified by the memory of Agamemnon [5], Elektra holds her ground. The exchange between mother and daughter that follows is one of the most remarkable in the opera.

4. Elektra and Klytemnestra

Klytemnestra's astonishing entry reveals how deeply (if unconsciously) she has comprehended Elektra's murderous impulses towards her; she herself is attempting to displace her guilt through repeated sacrifices to the gods. Before her, a procession of doomed cattle struggles its way to the slaughter, whips cracking in the air, the 'pagan' sonorities of motif [17] pressing it onwards inexorably. Her 'sallow, bloated', unspeakably weary appearance is rendered all the more grotesque by the burden of jewels that act as her talismans, and by the sinister presence of her confidante and train-bearer (they understand Elektra's wiles better than their mistress). The first part of the exchange is dominated by the soloistic figuration of [19b], a transformation of Elektra's taut figure [4a] that illustrates her 'darting tongue'. To the 'slaughter' motif [19c], Klytemnestra complains to the gods about the oppression she endures, and the aridity of her life [20]; but the fact that the music has absorbed the qualities of Elektra's harmonies points unerringly to the source of her anguish.

In the Greeks, the issue now becomes more complex. At the opening of her posthumous essay 'Some Reflections on the *Oresteia*' (1963), Klein analyses Klytemnestra's predicament according to Aeschylus:

> Klytemnestra justifies her murder as a revenge for the sacrifice of Iphigenia. For Iphigenia had been killed on Agamemnon's command in order to make the winds favourable for the voyage to Troy. [Agamemnon has in fact brought this disaster upon himself by carelessly shooting a stag belonging to the huntress Artemis.] Klytemnestra's revenge on Agamemnon, however, is not only caused by the grief for her child. She has, during his absence, taken his arch-enemy as her lover, and is therefore confronted with the fear of Agamemnon's revenge. It is clear that either Klytemnestra and her lover will be killed, or that she has to kill her husband.

In Sophocles too, the sacrifice of Iphigenia and the presence of Aegisthus form the main debating points between mother and daughter. Hofmannsthal, on the other hand, concentrates exclusively on Klytemnestra's attempt to mollify Elektra.

Klein found that, in adults as in very young children, there could coexist even with a 'ruthless and persecuting super-ego' a 'relation to the loved and even idealised parent' (she defines super-ego as 'the basis for the moral law which is ubiquitous in humanity'). At the start of their confrontation, the weary [14b] Klytemnestra acts upon a comparable perception to recall, in a low vocal register to the motif of the good family [10a], the time when Elektra knew her as the good mother she remembers herself to have been ('Das klingt mir so bekannt ...'). Initially, Elektra seems inscrutable [20]. Yet, to a consoling, rocking figure [21], she succeeds in luring her mother [6] away from her protesting attendants (who, according to the resentful [22] Klytemnestra, merely aggravate her misery with conflicting counsels and macabre visions, and hence compel her to ever more sacrifices [19c]). Strauss is at his most inventively illustrative in both this and the next, contrasting passage when, to the comforting figure [21], Klytemnestra announces she will bare her soul to her daughter like a sick man exposing his wounds to the balmy air. Her need for her good motherhood to be recognized is so desperate that she throws caution to the winds, dismisses her attendants and draws nearer to Elektra. Her jewels clink [23].

68

Kerstin Meyer as Klytemnestra at Covent Garden, 1975 (photo: Donald Southern)

Any illusion that the family situation could be redeemed is shattered by the ensuing, long (Wagnerian) transition from the extremes of Klytemnestra's opening tenderness to that of Elektra's closing viciousness. This need not have been the case: uninhibited confessions are necessary for the abreactions that restore health. But the force of Elektra's unforgiving, unreasoning hatred is profoundly disturbing (and will later shock even Orestes). This scene is as protracted as it is partly because Elektra gains a sadistic satisfaction by only slowly revealing to her mother her conviction that Orestes will return as Agamemnon's avenger, and partly because Klytemnestra resolutely resists acknowledging what she has already comprehended (the depth and substance of Elektra's feelings) until she absolutely has to.

Musically, the scene is supported by a rich blend of illustrative music, complex harmony (of this, more later) and motifs that reflect both aspects of the situation. For example, when Klytemnestra asks her 'intelligent' daughter what remedies she might know for bad dreams [24a], Elektra merely replies 'Do you have dreams, mother?' Although the orchestra belies her false naievety by recalling the Agamemnon motif [5], the retribution motif [9] and the Orestes-dream motif itself [18], Klytemnestra takes encouragement from Elektra's response, and the motif of consolation [21] is expanded as she attempts to enlist her daughter's help. There are other ironic uses of motif. Klytemnestra describes the oppressive effect of her sleeplessness with a figure [24b] derived from the dotted-note motif [13] that previously referred to the axe with which she slaughtered Agamemnon. This takes on another guise [24a] as she describes how her every limb clamours for death, and yet another [24c] as she begs Elektra to bring her visions to an end.

As matters gather to a head, the range of motivic reference expands. Elektra presses her advantage, and motifs from her earlier soliloquy are recapitulated: the victory dance [11], the good family [10] (used here defiantly as the topic of Orestes' whereabouts is broached), her own tensions [4a], both sets of Agamemnon motifs [1a, b and c, and 5], the axe [13] and retribution [9]. Two new ideas are introduced to support Elektra's effort to gain ascendancy: the first is a vicious little motif [y from 25a] that infiltrates the musical textures before taking its place in the predatory four-bar motif that subsequently seems to spring out at Klytemnestra; the second is the primitive, brazenly assertive figure [25b] that proclaims Elektra's indomitable will. Correspondingly, as Klytemnestra moves to the defensive, a recapitulation of her motifs — the Orestes dream [18], her nervous appearance [6], her authority [14a and b] and her impatience [24a] — is matched by an ominous expansion of the 'jewel' chords (and tonality) [23] as she threatens Elektra with torture.

One other striking point emerges from Elektra's concluding maledictions. She imagines pursuing Klytemnestra murderously through the house and coming upon her father seated in the darkness, unaware of the acts of retribution being performed around him. This joyless mental image of the dead father, so much at odds with that of the 'good family' Elektra invokes elsewhere, anticipates the dénouement. Since, metaphorically speaking, Agamemnon will claim them both as victims, there is an especial irony in Elektra's prophecy to her mother: 'then you will dream no more, and I shall have no more need for dreaming.'

The interlude (a kind of scherzo) accompanying the next vertiginous series of events both offers a contrast to what has gone before, and depicts the wild joy with which Klytemnestra greets the (false) news that Orestes is dead. This news has been brought by the maids and confidantes [26a]; the palace is illuminated [26b]; Klytemnestra and her entourage sweep out, leaving Elektra confused and ignorant; Chrysothemis, 'howling like a wild beast' [27], arrives; to the most harmonically anguished and chromatic presentation of the 'good family' motif [10], Elektra denies the truth of what she hears; Chrysothemis also reports the arrival of two strangers who have told how Orestes was dragged to death by his horses; a short, intense orchestral threnody combines an expansion of the 'grief' figure [27a] with Chrysothemis' [12]; a young slave rushes in, calling for a horse, so that he can tell Aegisthus (who is temporarily absent from the palace); Elektra and Chrysothemis find themselves left alone once more to contemplate a situation that appears to have changed dramatically in their mother's favour.

5. Elektra and Chrysothemis
In this and the next section, the opera addresses the sexual basis of the 'feelings and fantasies' which Jung was to ascribe to the Elektra complex. Its particular concern is to show how the powerfully life-enhancing erotic forces are entwined with equally powerful murderous ones. Elektra begins by insisting to Chrysothemis that it is now their responsibility to wield the axe upon their mother (Elektra's rapid, scheming motif [29] has taken over the urgency of the callow young slave's [28]); repeatedly, Chrysothemis calls for restraint [30]. The music resumes the brisk tempo, the triple time, the tonality, the lyrical manner and motifs of their previous confrontation, with one crucial difference. Whereas this music was sung before by Chrysothemis, it has now been appropriated by Elektra [31]. Standing oppressively close to

Chrysothemis, Elektra extols her sister's strength, ascribing it to the nights Chrysothemis spends as a virgin (Elektra's sexual experience is alluded to in the next section). It is this strength which, in Elektra's view, makes her the more eligible of the two to perform the deadly act of retribution. Speaking ever more like Salome, Elektra dwells with envy upon her sister's physical attributes. It is as if she wants to rediscover vicariously her own maidenhood, to begin her own sexual life again. Yet such a rediscovery could only be achieved through the murder of Klytemnestra.

Just as in the earlier encounter, Chrysothemis' vehemence testified to the hopelessness of arguing with Elektra, so here does Elektra's extravagant attention ensure that Chrysothemis is alienated. Elektra promises to project her entire being into her sibling, parading as she does so a humility that offers love but barely conceals its latent aggression and even guilt. To a poignant song (based on both [10a] and [10b]), she imagines waiting with Chrysomethis for her bridegroom, anointing him when he comes, and hiding her sister's maidenly blushes in her own breast. She proposes to act as the newly-weds' maidservant [2c], and eventually to lift their firstborn high into the air. When Chrysothemis [12] registers horror at all this, Elektra merely marvels at the beauty of her angry lips from which she longs to hear cries of retribution. As they begin to struggle, Elektra's motif of unresolved tension surfaces once more [4a], and, as Chrysothemis flees, Elektra curses her to an awesome statement of the Agamemnon motif [5]. With her prospects of vicarious sexual gratification apparently in ruins, Elektra falls to the earth and, adopting a position of extreme self-contempt, begins to dig under (and into) the palace 'like a wild beast'.

6. Elektra and Orestes

Whereas the previous section culminated in the disintegration of Elektra's hopes of any concerted action, this one prepares for, and documents her response to, the prospect of a full sexual and psychological reintegration. Orestes' return from exile poses all kinds of challenge for her: she must overcome the shocks of recognition, of coming dramatically into contact once more with the cherished past, of rationalising the intervening years for Orestes' benefit, and of adjusting to the present, with all the implications for the future which that entails. Each challenge is dealt with at some length.

Two aspects of the musical treatment in the opening stages reveal Strauss's priorities in handling the entire scene. On the one hand, the orchestral portrait of Elektra's burrowing gathers together her 'darting animal' motif [3], the retribution figure [9] and her scheming motif [29]; later two nervously taut ideas also relate to her physical condition [36a and b]. Together, these motifs establish the topic of her nervous state, which is developed later as she reveals her attitudes to her own body. On the other hand, several earlier motifs are reintroduced with 'pathetic' chromatic alteration to establish the spirit of desolation that greets Orestes upon his return [33a]. These include that of Agamemnon's 'psychological presence' in the palace [1 becoming 32a], and the 'good family' [10 becoming 32b]. When Elektra first asks Orestes who he is, the three solemnly portentous chords that accompany his reply support another plangent ('auxiliary note') figure [34] which in turn provides the motif of the ensuing exchange [33b]. A reference by Elektra to her brother's alleged death introduces yet another drooping figure [35].

Recognition itself is achieved, by contrast, with the help of three new motifs, and then only gradually. The first is a brisk figure [37] introduced when

71

Orestes realizes that he is talking to his sister (its second element (b) is skilfully blended with the other motifs currently in use). The second is a pregnant, nervous figure in the bass, heard first to the revelation 'Orestes lives' [39a], and more assertively when Orestes prepares himself for the murder. The third assumes a more important role as the principal idea of Elektra's recognition-song [38]. In the Austro–German symphonic tradition, important structural moments are often preceded by preparatory passages which foreshadow what is to come. So it is here. In the preparatory passage, motif [38] is heard as attendants rush in to kiss the hands and feet of Orestes (they recognize him before Elektra does); the unstable harmony and inclusion of other motifs in the passage characterize Elektra's confusion. The moment of recognition itself is much the most violent emotional experience for her in the opera, and releases such extreme harmonic tensions (derived from [3]) in the braying orchestra, that it takes a further 44 bars before a resolution into a stable tonality can be achieved.

Like many closed forms in music drama, Elektra's extraordinarily tender song inhabits a world significantly separated from surrounding events. Her words, which speak of dream visions and a readiness to expire in the glow of happiness brought on by the god-like figure who has appeared before her, could be those of a Wagnerian heroine. Indeed, the music is redolent of the point in Act Two of *Tristan und Isolde* where a leitmotif promises love's fulfilment in the peace of death:

EXAMPLE 1

The issue here is not that simple. The name upon which Elektra lingers so dotingly is that of her brother, although the song is not basically incestuous. The mature erotic feelings that pervade it have much more to do with her reclamation of the confidence that accompanied her infantile emotions of love and security. It is therefore highly significant that the coda to, and goal of, the song is a full presentation of the 'good family' idea [10]. Although Elektra sings her gratitude to Orestes, she is celebrating the restored images of 'good father' and 'good mother'.

Yet how great is the division in Elektra's mind between these images recovered from the past and the perilous present becomes at once apparent in the next exchange, which takes us to the heart of Jung's 'complex'. Orestes bends forward to embrace his sister [37] but, as the plangent motifs from earlier in the section return [32a and 33b], he is vehemently repulsed. Elektra is ashamed of her body, and launches into a confession (which includes some of the opera's most ravishing music). Sadly [33b] she recalls the time when she felt herself to be the king's daughter [5], when she exposed her beautiful body to the moon's flattering rays, when her hair made men tremble. From the orchestra we learn that it is her awareness of her dead father [1b] that has caused the same hair to grow unkempt and matted. As she relates the loss of her virginity, both sets of Agamemnon motif [1 and 5] echo in the music, with the figures of grief [27] and plangency [33b]. Most appallingly for her, is the fact that her love-making itself ('wenn ich an meinem Leib mich freute') is spoiled by the groans [1b and 33b] that seem to emanate from Agamemnon. It is this bondage, she explains, which has cast 'hollow-eyed hate' as her

Danica Mastilovic as Elektra with Norman Bailey as Orestes, Covent Garden, 1975 (photo: Donald Southern)

perpetual bridegroom, and which is responsible for the unresolved tensions [4a] that make her a source of constant terror and despair for others.

In the brief climax, Elektra regains her confidence. Orestes, overcoming his revulsion at her story (all his limbs are quaking [39a] by the end) also steels himself for the liberating deed, to an energetic and indomitable new motif [39b]. Elektra's blessing [40] rings in his ears: the motifs of the good family, the victory dance and the recognition song abound. The dénouement is set to unfold.

7. The Dénouement

The final section is constructed according to two principles, which together articulate the astonishing outcome to the tragedy as a whole. On the one hand is a traditional (Mozartian) finale, that subsumes several subsidiary sections in a hectic drive towards the conclusion. In the company of his tutor, Orestes gains admission to the palace, murders first Klytemnestra and then Aegisthus (who makes a timely return to the palace), before enjoying a triumphal (off-stage) reception from Chrysothemis and the maidservants. On the other hand, there is a Wagnerian peroration that charts the macabre ending of Elektra's blighted existence. This both contrasts with, and denies the joy and optimism of, the concurrent conventional finale by underlining just how far adrift from the others Elektra has become. There are three outstanding events: Elektra's frenzy during her mother's murder; her confrontation with Aegisthus; and, following her final encounter with Chrysothemis, her dance of death. And it is this death that will raise fascinating psychological issues.

The first two subsidiary sections concern Elektra and Klytemnestra. To a brutally murderous new motif [41], the tutor enters, scolding Orestes and Elektra for their noisy excitement [39]. Mindful of the dead Agamemnon [1b], of the strength that the recognition of brother and sister has given them [38], and of the destiny that is theirs to fulfil [34], they await the emergence of the maidservants and their lights [26a and b]. After a moment of repose in which he steels himself for the deed, Orestes enters the palace with the tutor. Left alone, Elektra springs frantically around the stage, once more 'like a trapped animal', with an appropriate array of motifs in the orchestra depicting her extreme nervous tension [25a, 29, 4a and 3]. When Klytemnestra's death-cry is heard from within, Elektra shrieks in sympathy [25a, 9], exorcising the 'bad mother' under whose shadow she has lived for so long.

Confusion reigns. Together with Chrysothemis, the servants pour in (to a transformation of motif [2c]). They suspect murder, and are alarmed by the silent stance Elektra has assumed [5]. As the sinister psychological presence of Agamemnon is reafirmed in the music [1a], they hear Aegisthus returning. At Chrysothemis's command, they hurry back into the palace in trepidation [41b]. Darkness falls once more.

The next phase of the finale also represents Elektra's last confrontation. Aegisthus enters, to an expanded version of his ineffectual, nonchalant motif [7]. The darkness alarms him [41b]. Elektra finds light and bows before him obsequiously. Her inner attitude, however, is conveyed by the fatal motif [18] which originated in Klytemnestra's dream of retribution at the hands of Orestes. This motif discreetly pervades the ensuing exchanges, later in the company of a rhythmic figure derived from the victory motif [11]. As Elektra tells Aegisthus of the two men who await him, her assumed politeness is deftly characterised in the orchestra: for its principal idea, the grief motif [27] is transformed into an ironic waltz tune [27b], to which a bland reworking of Elektra's motif of unresolved tension acts as a counter-melody. Even the choice of tonality, the E♭ major previously associated with Chrysothemis' hopes of life, love and family, mocks Aegisthus: and as he enters the palace, it eerily slips into the tonality associated with the motif of brutality introduced with the arrival of the tutor at the beginning of the section [41a and b]. Aegisthus' murder is more protracted than was Klytemnestra's. His pleas for help are countered only by Elektra's motif of defiance [25b] and her cry 'Agamemnon hears you' to the work's very opening idea [1a], cast in the tonality of retribution (C minor). Clearly, Elektra's cry represents the final, triumphant defence of the image of the good father over his evil and craven usurper. But it also represents a strenghtening of the bond between Elektra and Agamemnon, a bond which in the last phase of the dénouement, Elektra, fatally, will be unable to sever.

Leonie Rysanek as Elektra in the film directed by Götz Friedrich and designed by Josef Svoboda and Pet Halmen, Production Unitel, 1982

Indeed, it is in the work's closing stages that the two principles of construction found in this section are most sharply focused: Chrysothemis and Elektra celebrate the murders in opposite ways. The spirit of elation that accompanies Chrysothemis' arrival — another textural and tonal contrast with preceding events — is explained in the music: her pleas to Elektra [30] are combined with the recognition motif (she too has met Orestes), and the figure of grief now reappears transformed into one of celebration [27c]. Cries of joy emanate from the palace, as Orestes receives a hero's welcome: in due course these are supported in the orchestra by the motif of comfort (from the confrontation with Klytemnestra) [21] and the opening Agamemnon theme

[1], both ideas now purged of their ironic or sinister overtones. After a brief report of the battle that has raged within between the supporters of Orestes and Aegisthus [39, 41a, 32a and 41b], Elektra steps forward to bring the celebrations to a head, with the claim that the music of rejoicing 'comes from' her: all are waiting for her to 'lead the dance' [4, 11, 38, 10]. Yet, in one of the work's most dramatic reversals, she finds she cannot act as such a leader. As the motif of grief rises up crushingly once more [27], she complains that it is as if 'the weight of the ocean' was bearing down on her limbs. Chrysothemis, however, is beside herself with excitement, and pays no attention to her sister. In the duets both sing as if to themselves. Chrysothemis is ecstatic at what seems a god-given promise of a new order [10]; Elektra characteristically identifies herself with the gods who salute accomplishment [39b], and claims that she is physically transformed: her face now gleams whiter than the moonlight. Both sisters sing of the necessity of love. Only Elektra senses its destructiveness.

Whereas earlier Elektra found herself incapable of leading the dance that would restore social dignity, she now breaks into her own wild death dance. The stage instruction here significantly recalls Nietzsche's description in *The Birth of Tragedy* of the rival forces of order (Apollo) and disorder (Dionysos): Elektra is to behave like a maenad. (In classical mythology, maenads were women who surrendered themselves entirely to the primeval urges of nature, having first been raised into a frenzy by Dionysos.) The motifs in the music appropriately jumble together Elektra's contradictory feelings of ghoulish triumph [11], vindication [39b], tension [4a], confidence born of recognition [38] and the love emanating from her memory of the good family. Chrysothemis as ever urges restraint [30]: Elektra calls for the others to follow her example. Suddenly, the music accelerates, the axe and retribution motifs blaze through the orchestra, and Elektra falls lifeless. The spirit of Agamemnon [1] reaffirms itself imposingly: his dark grip upon his daughter has prevailed. Chrysothemis calls hopelessly and in anguish to Orestes, the liberator, restorer of order and symbol of the good family. But the fragmentation of the texture and harmony in the closing bars of the opera testify to the strength of the forces that have prevented the triumph of conventional order. The inert (E♭ minor) death chords of Elektra are pitted against the grimly exulting (C minor) harmonies supporting the Agamemnon motif. And although the resolution of these C minor harmonies into the clear closing C major could be construed as affirming a confident future for Chrysothemis and the other survivors, this is not the effect of the music. Rather, the brusque ending, in which E♭ and C harmonies are still bound together in succession, seems to offer little comfort.

Such an ending raises many questions. Why did Elektra have to die? Why is she not purged by the murders? What compulsion has allowed her death instincts to gain so resounding a victory over her life forces? Is she like a certain kind of child that Klein identifies, unable to accept 'gratification when it follows on deprivation'? Is she, indeed, as Sophocles' chorus accuses her early in his play, a 'hoarder of grief' whose 'sullen soul breeds strife unending', a temperament which finds fulfilment in precisely the psychological trap in which it is caught? Or should one assume that the most important determining factors in her death are the ones she never mentions, as might be the assumption in clinical psychiatry? Is she, for example, powerfully motivated by sibling rivalry for her (virgin) sister Iphigenia, whose sacrifice by her father constituted a kind of rape? In other words, must Elektra too be sacrificed? How else could Elektra's 'internalized dead object', Agamemnon, have maintained so threatening and fatal a hold upon her? And if something of this kind is not true, why should both the text and the music of the opera dwell so powerfully on both the sexual and sensual nature of things?

The work is not a staged case history. And the fact that it makes no attempt to provide answers to the problems it poses, but instead describes the sensational effects of concealed causes, lays bare its aesthetic aims. What is celebrated here is the mystery of the dark workings of the mind, and their relation to the awesomely destructive and self-destructive energies of nature.

The Musical Innovations

The relation between the musical innovations of *Elektra* and the dramatic and psychological ones must be understood in the context of Strauss's indebtedness to Wagner in four areas of thought: key association, key relation, functional tonality, and the absorption of an alternative repertoire of new chords. In each of these areas, Strauss was able to build significantly upon his legacy.

The fact that many of the work's principal tonalities come in internally contrasted tonic major/minor pairs suggests parallels with the dramatic contrasts. The opening tonality is a case in point. This D minor not merely establishes the doom-laden atmosphere of the first section, but is heard again with Chrysothemis' cry 'Orest is dead' as a motivic tonality, later defines the first chord of Orestes' motif [34] ('I have to wait here'), and finally inaugurates the dénouement, with the tutor's arrival. On the other hand, the few startling references to Wagner's numinous key of D major reinforce Elektra's conviction that 'Orestes is coming' to set matters aright. It is also the key of the passage in which she imagines holding up Chrysothemis' first-born, after hearing the false news of Orestes' death. The latent connection in her mind becomes manifest through this tonal association: if Orestes is dead, a new life must take his place.

There are other comparable pairings. Bb major denotes Elektra's royal past, and is used most poignantly as she sings to Orestes of her former beauty. On the other hand, Bb minor opens the second section to convey her sullen fury that this past is being wilfully ignored. Later in this section, this Bb major/minor duality is distilled into the motif of the imaginary victory dance over the graves of Klytemnestra and Aegisthus [11]. It has already been shown how Eb major is the key to which Chrysothemis [12] sings of her hopes for life and love [16], and how this Eb major returns significantly in sections 5 and 7. By contrast, Eb minor is used for the threnody [27] which encloses the false announcement of Orestes' death, and again at the end of the opera for the chords to which Elektra herself dies. Whereas E minor represents adversarial stealth (coloured in [20] by the tritone Bb), a stealth that comes to the fore at the opening of section 6 as Elektra begins to burrow into the palace, E major projects the sublime happiness that comes with sibling recognition [27 and 37c]. This E major is also used ironically as Elektra extends false comfort to Klytemnestra early in section 4. (Its traditional alternative use as a bright, busy key comes with the entry of the maidservants towards the end of this section [26].) C minor [9 and 25] consistently threatens retribution; C major [40] resolves this fear. Aegisthus lives by F major, and meets his death to F minor. Further examples could be found.

Tonalities are brought into opposition through a network of key-relations.

The theorist Tovey used to refer to such relations as aesthetic 'facts', since certain effects could always be guaranteed once particular chords (and by extension the keys associated with them) were placed beside each other. He saw the most extreme opposition to lie between the 'unrelated' tonalities separated by the interval of an augmented fourth (the 'tritone'). It is these especially that are exploited in *Elektra*. The portentous D minor of the opening, for example, stands at a tritone relation to the Ab major of the 'recognition song' heard in section 6. In section 4, however, these two keys are dramatically juxtaposed. To a strained (diminished) version of the comfort motif [21] heard over a sustained D (from [18]), Klytemnestra tries to gain her daughter's attention. Abruptly, but quietly, Elektra subverts her enquiry by asking what plans Klytemnestra has for Orestes. This enquiry is set to the good family motif [10] in Ab major.

Such an aggressive use of the tritone is not peculiar to Strauss: one may find comparable things in Wagner (Siegfried's death in *Götterdämmerung*, for instance) or Bizet (Carmen's G major challenge to the Db major of Don José's Flower Song). Strauss's advance lay in his fusion of tritone-related chords to create motifs expressive of psychological or physical anguish. This is especially the case with the B minor and F minor chords. B minor is associated with the ubiquitous threat of violence, when Klytemnestra attempts to intimidate Elektra ('und aus dir bring ich . . .'), and when Orestes rests before committing the murders (one may also compare Klytemnestra's jewel motif [27]). The combination of this B minor with the even more portentous F minor creates the motif of Elektra's animal movements [3], which in turn Klytemnestra introjects, so to speak, to produce her motif of frenzy [24]. In this latter motif, the two chords are superimposed. Then again, F# major, the key through which Klytemnestra establishes her grip on the palace [14a and b], stands at the furthest remove from C major, the tonality which resolves the (C minor) forces of retribution. In section 4, a remarkable progression shows that the direct outcome of this conflict between a superimposed F# major [14a] and C major/minor is the terror symbolised by B minor and F minor (Example 2):

EXAMPLE 2

Throughout the opera, there are also interlocked triads set apart at the interval of a minor third. At the opening, Elektra's motif of unresolved tensions [4a and b] forms the perspective from which she views Klytemnestra [6] and Aegisthus [7]; at the end, Agamemnon's grimly triumphant C minor is juxtaposed with the Eb minor of Elektra's death chords. One of the most significant progressions from these interlocked triads is shown in motif [8b]. Here, the last chord, marked with an asterisk, is derived from a whole-tone scale, and supports Elektra's description of the slaughter to come. Whole-tone chords belong to the alternative types of harmony that Strauss developed far beyond what Wagner had attempted, and are associated throughout the opera with gruesome images of death. They are found in motif [13], the axe figure, and also in motif [8a], where such chords move in parallel to illustrate the dragging of Agamemnon's bloody body through the palace. They can also dominate extended stretches of music, most remarkably with Klytemnestra's account of the horror that grips her ('es ist kein Wort'). Other alternative chordal types used illustratively include augmented harmonies which refer to Klytemnestra's sacrifices [19c]; bare fifths suggestive of her ominous machinations [15 and 17]; diminished harmonies which not only convey distress in the usual way (as in the Orestes-dream motif [18]) but appear more insidiously in the bass line of Klytemnestra's motif of domination [14a]; and there are further examples.

Within this context, the relatively straightforward functional tonality that underpins Chrysothemis' plea for life and love [16a] assumes a distinct colour of its own; the bass line simply ascends from tonic to dominant. And this use of tonality, expanded in section 5 particularly by many harmonic and enharmonic excursions, contrasts with another, specifically Romantic exploration of key, where chord and line may stand in meaningful contradiction. In Elektra's motif of defiance [25b], for instance, the bass notes outline a chord of C major, whereas the harmonies they support are those of G major, C minor and E major. From this point of view, one might also compare the retribution motif [9].

This discussion may suggest that listening to, or studying, the music of *Elektra* simply entails ascribing metaphorical significance to its readily identifiable elements. This is not the case, and the analytical task is far harder. There are many other, purely musical processes that are also engaged. Even the orchestration creates large-scale contrasts of its own, and the overall formal design is loosely redolent of the symphonic principles found in the tone poems (principles upon which Schoenberg also drew for works such as the Chamber Symphony Op. 9). If section 1 is an introduction, for example, then sections 2 and 3 contain the first and second groups of ideas respectively; section 4 combines development (particularly from a harmonic point of view), recapitulation of the first group of ideas and its B♭ major tonality as Elektra reveals her attitudes to Klytemnestra, and an interrupting scherzo as the maidservants burst in; section 5 recapitulates and develops Chrysothemis' music from section 3 (the second group of ideas); section 6 contains a slow movement of a kind (Elektra's recognition song), and section 7 gathers most of these threads into a conclusion. If the purely musical organisation shows the limitations of bringing psychologically-derived metaphors to bear on opera, it also demonstrates the richness of ideas that between them Strauss and Hofmannsthal engaged. It may also explain something of the work's enduring fascination.

[handwritten margin note: symphonic structure – plausible]

I am grateful to Dr Gerald Wooster and his colleagues in the Department of Psychiatry, St George's Hospital (University of London), Tooting, for their stimulating reactions to an earlier version of this essay. Citations from Jung are drawn from the Collected Works, Volume 4, Routledge, London, 1961, pp. 151–156. The essay by Melanie Klein is included in Volume III of her writings, *Envy and Gratitude and Other Works 1946–1963*, the Hogarth Press, London, 1975. I have also drawn ideas from other essays in this volume. The quotation from Freud and Breuer is taken from their chapter 'On the Psychical Mechanism of Hysterical Phenomena' in *Studies in Hysteria*, Volume 3, Penguin Freud Library, London, 1974, p. 62. (The chapter was first published in 1893.)

Thematic Guide

Many of the themes from *Elektra* have been identified in the articles by numbers in square brackets, which refer to the themes set out in these pages. The themes are also identified by the numbers in square brackets at the corresponding points in the libretto, so that the words can be related to the musical themes.

murder music 6 + 7.

demand for.
retribution motif..

walz theme

[11]
Kräftig bewegt

[12]
Etwas breit

[13]
Lebhaft

[14a]

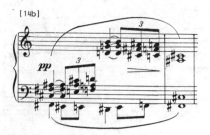

[14b]

82

[15]

coll' 8va bassa

Chrysothemis

[16a]
Sehr lebhaft

[16b]

[16c]
Ruhig

etc.

[17]
Sehr schnell

pp

[18]
Sehr schnell

[19a]
Sehr schnell

f sfz

[19b]

[19c]
Langsamer

83

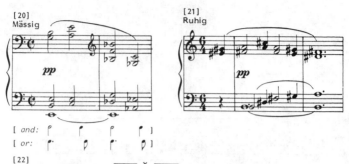

[20]
Mässig
pp

[21]
Ruhig
pp

[and: ♩ ♩ ♩ ♩]
[or: ♩. ♪ ♩. ♪]

[22]
Schnell und heftig

[23]
Mässig

[24a]
Bewegter

[24b]
mf   fp

[24c]
p

[25a]
Sehr schnell
fff

[25b]

[26a]
Sehr schnell
8va

[26b]

85

[35]

[36a]

[36b]

[37a]
Noch lebhafter

[37b]

[38]
Mässig bewegt

[39a]
Lebhaft

[39b]

[40]
Sehr lebhaft

[41a]
Schnell und heftig

[41b]

Elektra

Tragedy in One Act
by Hugo von Hofmannsthal
Music by Richard Strauss
English version by Anthony Hose

Elektra was first performed at the Hofoper, Dresden, on January 25, 1909. It was first performed in the USA at the Manhattan Opera, New York, on February 1, 1910. The first performance in Britain was at Covent Garden on February 19, 1910.

Birgit Nilsson as Elektra in the Covent Garden production by Rudolf Hartmann, designed by Isabel Lambert (photo: Zoë Dominic)

CHARACTERS

Klytemnestra	*mezzo-soprano*
Elektra ⎫ *her daughters*	*soprano*
Chrysothemis ⎭	*soprano*
Aegisthus	*tenor*
Orestes	*baritone*
The Tutor of Orestes	*bass*
The Confidante	*soprano*
The Trainbearer	*soprano*
A Young Servant	*tenor*
An Old Servant	*bass*
The Overseer	*soprano*
Five Maid Servants	*contralto, sopranos, mezzo-sopranos*

Servants

The action takes place in Mycenae.

Klytemnestra (Helga Dernesch) calls for more lights in the production by August Everding, designed by Mauro Pagano at the Cologne Opera, 1983 (photo: Paul Leclaire)

The inner courtyard, bounded by the back of the palace, and low buildings in which the servants live.
Maid servants at the well at the front of the stage to the left. Overseers are among them. [1a]

FIRST MAID SERVANT
(lifting her pitcher)

Where is Elektra?

Wo bleibt Elektra?

SECOND MAID SERVANT

Now it is her moment,
the moment she bewails her father so
that every wall re-echoes.

Ist doch ihre Stunde,
die Stunde, wo sie um den Vater heult,
[2a] dass alle Wände schallen.

Elektra runs out of the entrance hall, which is already growing dark within. All turn to look at her.
Elektra darts back like an animal to its lair, one arm held in front of her face. [3, 4a]

FIRST MAID SERVANT

Did you not see the way she watched
us?

Habt ihr gesehn, wie sie uns ansah?

SECOND MAID SERVANT

Spiteful,
just like a wild cat's look.

Giftig,
wie eine wilde Katze.

THIRD MAID SERVANT

Recently she lay there
groaning.

Neulich lag sie da
[1b] und stöhnte —

FIRST MAID SERVANT

Always, when the sun's low-lying,
she lies and groans.

Immer, wenn die Sonne tief steht,
liegt sie und stöhnt.

THIRD MAID SERVANT

The two of us went by,
but then we got too near.

Da gingen wie zu zweit
und kamen ihr zu nah —

FIRST MAID SERVANT

She can't abide
anyone to watch her.

Sie hält's nicht aus,
wenn man sie ansieht.

THIRD MAID SERVANT

Yes, and as we got
too near, she spat at us as any cat would
have
spat. 'Go, blowflies, go', she cried.

Ja, wir kamen ihr
zu nah. Da pfauchte sie wie eine Katze
uns an. 'Fort, Fliegen!' schrie sie, 'fort!'

FOURTH MAID SERVANT

'Bluebottles, go!'

[2b] 'Schmeissfliegen, fort!'

THIRD MAID SERVANT

'Don't sit upon my ulcers!'
And struck at us, using a wisp of straw.

'Sitzt nicht auf meinen Wunden!'
und schlug nach uns mit einem Strohwisch.

FOURTH MAID SERVANT

'Bluebottles, go!'

Schmeissfliegen, fort!'

THIRD MAID SERVANT

'You should not suck the soft
sweetness out of my pain. You should
not smack
your lips at my spasms' foam!'

'Ihr sollt das Süsse nicht
abweiden von der Qual. Ihr sollt nicht
schmatzen
nach meiner Krämpfe Schaum.'

FOURTH MAID SERVANT

'Away, crawl off now!'
she screamed at us; 'eat fat things and eat sweet
things, and go to bed with all your men!'
she shouted.
And she . . .

'Geht ab, verkriecht euch,'
schrie sie uns nach: 'Esst Fettes und esst Süsses
und geht zu Bett mit euren Männern,'
schrie sie,
und die —

THIRD MAID SERVANT

I was not slow.

Ich war nicht faul —

FOURTH MAID SERVANT

She gave her answer.

Die gab ihr Antwort!

THIRD MAID SERVANT

'Yes, when you need to eat,' I gave my answer,
'you eat as well!' Then up she sprang and shot
horrible glances, curling up her fingers
like claws towards us both, and cried: 'I'm fattening
up a vulture in my flesh!'

'Ja, wenn du hungrig bist,' gab ich zur Antwort,
'so isst du auch,' da sprang sie auf und schoss
grässliche Blicke, reckte ihre Finger
wie Krallen gegen uns und schrie: 'Ich füttre
mir einen Geier auf im Leib.'

SECOND MAID SERVANT

And you?

Und du?

THIRD MAID SERVANT

'That's why you always squat,' I answered
back, 'where carrion stench prevails, and scratch
for some old rotting carcass.'

'Drum hockst du immerfort,' gab ich
zurück, 'wo Aasgeruch dich hält, und scharrst
nach einer alten Leiche!'

SECOND MAID SERVANT

And then, what did she say?

Und was sagt sie da?

THIRD MAID SERVANT

She howled and threw herself back
into her corner.

[1c] Sie heulte nur und warf sich
in ihren Winkel.

FIRST MAID SERVANT

That the Queen
allows such a demoniac creature free to wander
round her house and yard!

Dass die Königin
solch einen Dämon frei in Haus und Hof
sein Wesen treiben lässt.

SECOND MAID SERVANT

It's her own child!

Das eigne Kind!

FIRST MAID SERVANT

Were she my child I'd keep her,
— by God! —
I'd keep her barred and bolted!

Wär' sie mein Kind, ich hielte, ich —
bei Gott! —
[4b] sie unter Schloss und Riegel.

FOURTH MAID SERVANT

Aren't they
harsh enough with her for you? Do they not set
her bowl of food down with the dogs' food?
Have you not seen the master beating her?

Sind sie dir
nicht hart genug mit ihr? Setzt man ihr nicht
[2c] den Napf mit Essen zu den Hunden?
Hast du den Herrn nie sie schlagen sehn?

FIFTH MAID SERVANT
(quite young, with trembling, agitated voice)

I shall
throw down myself before her, and her feet
I shall kiss. Is she not a king's own child,
yet suffers such disgrace? I shall anoint
her feet and then with my own hair I'll [5]
dry them.

Ich will
vor ihr mich niederwerfen und die Füsse
ihr küssen. Ist sie nicht ein Königskind
und duldet solche Schmach? Ich will die Füsse
ihr salben und mit meinem Haar sie
trocknen.

OVERSEER
(pushing her)

Inside with you!

Hinein mit dir!

FIFTH MAID SERVANT

There is nothing on earth
in aspect as royal as she. She lies
in rags upon the threshold, and yet no one,
nobody in this house, can even meet her glance!

Es gibt nichts auf der Welt,
das königlicher ist als sie. Sie liegt
in Lumpen auf der Schwelle, aber niemand,
niemand ist hier im Haus, der ihren Blick aushält!

OVERSEER
(pushing her through the open, low doorway to the left downstage)

Get in!

Hinein!

FIFTH MAID SERVANT
(caught in the doorway)

Not one of you is fit
to breathe the same air that she breathes. [2d]
Oh,
could I see you all, all, strung up by the gullet
in some foul gloomy cowshed, hanging there
in reparation for all that Elektra's endured!

Ihr alle seid nicht wort,
die Luft zu atmen, die sie atmet! O,
könnt' ich euch alle, euch, erhängt am Halse,
in einer Scheuer Dunkel hängen sehn
um dessenwillen, was ihr an Elektra getan!

OVERSEER
(She slams the door.)

Do you hear? Us, for Elektra,
who pushed her bowl away from where we ate
when she was told to eat with us. Who then spat
at us, and called us each one bitches?

Hört ihr das? Wir, an Elektra,
die ihren Napf von unserm Tische stiess,
als man mit uns sie essen hiess, die ausspie
vor uns und Hündinnen uns nannte.

FIRST MAID SERVANT

What?
She said there is no dog could be degraded
to equal us in degradation, that we must
wash away with endless pails of water
the eternal blood of murder from this royal
household.

Was?
Sie sagte: keinen Hund kann man erniedern,
wozu man uns hat abgerichtet: dass wir
mit Wasser und mit immer frischem Wasser
das ewige Blut des Mordes von der Diele
abspülen.

THIRD MAID SERVANT

'And the shame,' she always says,
'the shame which every day and night is renewed,
we sweep in a corner.'

'Und die Schmach,' so sagte sie,
'die Schmach, die sich bei Tag und Nacht erneut,
in Winkel fegen . . .'

FIRST MAID SERVANT

'And our flesh', she cries,
'recoils at this excrement we're servile
to!'

'Unser Leib,' so schreit sie,
'starrt von dem Unrat, dem wir dienstbar
sind!'

The maids carry the pots into the building on the left.

OVERSEER
(who has opened the door for them)

And when she sees us with our children
here,
she shrieks out: 'None can be so damned,
none,
as children who we, cowering on the
blood-
covered slippery stairways, here, within
this house,
have conceived and suckled into being.'
Does she
say that or not?

Und wenn sie uns mit unsern Kindern
sieht,
so schreit sie: 'Nichts kann so verflucht
sein, nichts,
als Kinder, die wir hündisch auf der
Treppe
im Blute glitschernd, hier in diesem
Hause
empfangen und geboren haben.' Sagt sie
das oder nicht?

MAID SERVANTS
(as they go in)

Yes, yes.

Ja! Ja!

OVERSEER

Does she say that or not?

Sagt sie das oder nicht?

MAID SERVANTS
(within)

Yes, yes.

Ja! Ja!

The overseers go in; the door closes.

FIFTH MAID SERVANT
(within)

They're beating me!

[2d] Sie schlagen mich!

Elektra steps out of the building.

ELEKTRA

Alone! Ah, all alone! My father gone,
cast down below inside his icy cavern . . .

[4a] Allein! Weh, ganz allein. Der Vater fort,
hinabgescheucht in seine kalten Klüfte . . .

(with her eyes fixed upon the ground)

Agamemnon! Agamemnon!
Where are you, father? Have you not the
strength
to lift your face up here to me, your
daughter?

[1, 5] Agamemnon! Agamemnon!
Wo bist du, Vater? Hast du nicht die
Kraft,
dein Angesicht herauf zu mir zu schleppen?

(softly)

It is the moment, our most sacred
moment,
the moment when you were so foully
slaughtered
by her, your wife, and him, who sleep in
one bed,
in your own royal bed as man and wife.
They struck you in your bath to death,
your blood
ran over both your eyelids, and the bath
reeked of your steaming blood. He
seized you then,
the coward, by the shoulders, dragging
you
outside from the room, your head in
front,

Es ist die Stunde, unsre Stunde ist's,

die Stunde, wo sie dich geschlachtet haben,

[6] dein Weib und der mit ihr in einem Bette,

[7] in deinem königlichen Bette schläft.
Sie schlugen dich im Bade tot, dein Blut

rann über deine Augen, und das Bad
dampfte von deinem Blut. Da nahm er
dich,
[8a] der Feige, bei den Schultern, zerrte dich

hinaus aus dem Gemach, den Kopf
voraus,

your legs splaying out behind. Your eyes,
which were staring, open, gazed back in
the house.
So you'll return now, treading step by
step,
and suddenly stand there, your glistening
eyes
wide open, a royal wreath of shining
purple resting on your noble brow, which
feeds
itself upon your open headwound.
Agamemnon! Father!
I want to see you, do not leave me here
alone!
But just like yesterday, like a shadow in
the wall's dark corner, come before your
child.
Father! Agamemnon! Your day approaches!
From the heavens
gush all the seasons down, so will the
blood
of a hundred gullets gush down on your
grave!
As if from overturned pitchers blood will
from those shackled murderers flow out,
and in one great surge, in one mighty
swollen flood, their very life's existence
will from them gush out.

(uttered solemnly)
And we'll sacrifice
the stallions which are stabled here, we'll
drive
them out to your grave together, and
they'll sense
death at hand and whinny in death's
atmosphere
and die there. And we'll sacrifice the
hounds,
those which came and licked your feet,
those you hunted with, those for which
you threw down tit-bits, they must shed

their blood for you, and end their duties
thus, and we,
we your blood, your son Orest and your
two daughters,
we three, when all this is fulfilled and
purple canopies are raised up from the
fumes
of blood, which the sun has sucked
upwards,
then we, your blood, shall dance round
by your grave.

(in ecstatic pathos)
Over the corpses there I'll lift my legs
high up step by step, and they shall see

how I dance about, yes, those who are far
off
may only see just how my shadows
dance.
They will all say: 'Such a mighty
monarch's
here, for such festive pomp and
pageantry

die Beine schleifend hinterher: dein Auge,
das starre, offne, sah herein ins Haus.
[9] So kommst du wieder, setzest Fuss vor
Fuss
und stehst auf einmal da, die beiden Augen
weit offen, und ein königlicher Reif
von Purpur ist um deine Stirn, der speist
sich
aus des Hauptes offner Wunde.
Agamemnon! Vater!
Ich will dich sehn, lass mich heute nicht
allein!
Nur so wie gestern, wie ein Schatten, dort
[10] im Mauerwinkel zeig dich deinem Kind!
Vater! Agamemnon! Dein Tag wird
kommen! Von den Sternen
stürzt alle Zeit herab, so wird das Blut
aus hundert Kehlen stürzen auf dein
Grab!
So wie aus umgeworfnen Krügen wird's
aus den gebundnen Mördern fliessen,
und in einem Schwall, in einem
geschwollen Bach wird ihres Lebens Leben
[8b] aus ihnen stürzen

und wir schlachten dir
die Rosse, die im Hause sind, wir treiben
sie vor dem Grab zusammen, und sie ahnen
den Tod und wiehern in die Todesluft
und sterben. Und wir schlachten dir die
Hunde,
[11] die dir die Füsse leckten,
die mit dir gejagt, denen du
die Bissen hinwarfst, darum muss ihr
Blut
hinab, um dir zu Dienst zu sein, und wir,
wir,
dein Blut, dein Sohn Orest und deine
Töchter,
wir drei, wenn alles dies vollbracht und
Purpurgezelte aufgerichtet sind, vom
Dunst
des Blutes, den die Sonne nach sich zieht,
dann tanzen wir, dein Blut, rings um
dein Grab.

Und über Leichen hin werd' ich das Knie
hochleben Schritt für Schritt, und die
mich werden
so tanzen sehn, ja, die meinen Schatten
von weitem nur so werden tanzen sehn,
die werden sagen: einem grossen König
wird hier ein grosses Prunkfest angestellt

Erna Schlüter as Elektra and Annelies Kupper as Chrysothemis at Covent Garden in 1953 (Royal Opera House Archives)

is held by his flesh and blood, and happy
is he
with children, who round his holy grave
such royal dances of triumph dance.'
Agamemnon! Agamemnon!

von seinem Fleisch und Blut, und glücklich
ist,
wer Kinder hat, die um sein hohes Grab
so königliche Siegestänze tanzen!
[1d] Agamemnon! Agamemnon!

The younger sister stands in the doorway.

CHRYSOTHEMIS
(softly)

Elektra!   [30]   Elektra!

Elektra starts as though waking from a dream and gazes at Chrysothemis.

ELEKTRA

Ah, it's that face!   Ah, das Gesicht!

CHRYSOTHEMIS
(pressed against the door; she speaks calmly, gently)

Do you so hate to see my face?   Ist mein Gesicht dir so verhasst?

ELEKTRA
(vehemently)

What is it? Tell me, speak, discharge
yourself,
then go and leave me!

Was willst du? Rede, sprich, ergiesse
dich,
[12] dann geh und lass mich!

Chrysothemis lifts her hands as though to defend herself.

Why lift up your hands,   Was hebst du die Hände?
just as our father lifted up his two hands   So hob der Vater seine beiden Hände,
before the axe came down and split apart [13] da fuhr das Beil hinab und spaltete
his flesh? What is it, daughter of my   sein Fleisch. Was willst du? Tochter
                                          meiner
mother? Daughter of Klytemnestra? [14a, b] Mutter, Tochter Klytämnestras?

CHRYSOTHEMIS

They've something really terrible in   [15] Sie haben etwas Fürchterliches vor.
mind.

ELEKTRA

What, those two women?   Die beiden Weiber?

CHRYSOTHEMIS

Who?   Wer?

ELEKTRA

Why, my mother, [6]   Nun, meine Mutter
that other woman too, that coward, yes,   und jenes andre Weib, die Memme, ei,
Aegisth the brave heroic murderer, he [7] Aegisth, der tapfre Meuchelmörder, er,
whose valiant actions all take place in   der Heldentaten nur im Bett vollführt.
bed.
What do they plan to do?   Was haben sie denn vor?

CHRYSOTHEMIS

Imprison you   Sie werfen dich
inside a tower where you'll not see the   in einen Turm, wo du von Sonn' und
light   Mond
of sun or moon again.   [15] das Licht nicht sehen wirst.

Elektra laughs.

They will; I know it;   Sie tun's, ich weiss es,
I heard them talk.   ich hab's gehört.

ELEKTRA

How did you come to   Wie hast denn du
hear them talking?   es hören können?

CHRYSOTHEMIS
(whispering)

At the door, Elektra.   An der Tür, Elektra.

ELEKTRA
(bursting out)

Keep every door shut fast inside this house!   [8c] Mach keine Türen auf in diesem Haus!
Just stifled breathing, pah! and death rattles   Gepresster Atem, pfui! Und Röcheln von Erwürgten,
of the strangled — no other sounds are heard in these walls.   nichts andres gibt's in diesen Mauern!
Keep every door shut fast! Don't skulk around,   Mach keine Türen auf! Schleich nicht herum,
sit at the door like me, and wish for death   sitz an der Tür wie ich und wünsch den Tod
and early judgement on both her and him.   und das Gericht herbei auf sie und ihn.

CHRYSOTHEMIS

I cannot sit here staring into darkness   [16a] Ich kann nicht sitzen und ins Dunkel starren,
like you. I have a fire in my breast,   wie du. Ich hab's wie Feuer in der Brust,
it drives me constantly around the house.   es treibt mich immerfort herum im Haus;
In no room can I bear to stay, I move   in keiner Kammer leidet's mich, ich muss
on from one doorway to another. Ah!   von einer Schwelle auf die andre, ach!
Upstairs and down, it seems that someone calls.   Treppauf, treppab, mir ist, als rief es mich,
I hurry in to find an empty room staring   und komm' ich hin, so stiert ein leeres Zimmer
back. I'm gripped by such a fear, my legs   [1b] mich an. Ich habe solche Angst, mir zittern
won't stop shaking day and night. I feel my throat   die Knie bei Tag and Nacht, mir ist die Kehle
is choked up so much that I can't even cry,   wie zugeschnürt, ich kann nicht einmal weinen,
all's turned to stone! Sister, please have pity!   [12] wie Stein ist alles! Schwester, hab Erbarmen!

ELEKTRA

On whom?   [5] Mit wem?

CHRYSOTHEMIS

Your influence: like an iron clamp   Du bist es, die mit Eisenklammern
it rivets me firmly captive. But for you,   mich an den Boden schmiedet. Wärst nicht du,
they'd let us out of here. But for your hate,   sie liessen uns hinaus. Wär' nicht dein Hass,
your tireless, inexorable drive,   dein schlafloses, unbändiges Gemüt,
at which they tremble, ah, they'd surely   vor dem sie zittern, ach, so liessen sie
let us get away from this foul prison, sister!   uns ja heraus aus diesem Kerker, Schwester!
I must get out! I won't lie here each night   Ich will heraus! Ich will nicht jede Nacht
sleeping till death unchains me. Before dying,   bis an den Tod hier schlafen! Eh' ich sterbe,
I want to live first! I want to have children   will ich auch leben! Kinder will ich haben,
before my body wilts. Were it a peasant   bevor mein Leib verwelkt, und wär's ein Bauer,
whom they would give me, children I would   dem sie mich geben; Kinder will ich ihm
gladly bear him, and I'd warm them to my bosom   [16b] gebären und mit meinem Leib sie wärmen

on wintry nights, when the hut is shaken by
stormy weather.
Do you not hear? Speak to me, sister!

ELEKTRA

Poor little wretch!

CHRYSOTHEMIS
(the whole in extreme agitation)

Have pity on yourself now, and on me!
Who gains then from such pain?
Our father, he is dead. Our brother won't come home.
Always sitting here on our perches,
like captive birds we're waiting, turning left
and right our heads, and no one comes, no brother,
no envoy from our brother, nor the envoy
of an envoy. Nothing! Each day like a knife
engraves its mark on my face and on yours.
And here outside the sun goes up
and down, and women, once quite slender creatures,
now blessed with burdens, toil to the well
and scarce can lift their buckets, and then
all at once they're released from their great load.
When next they come to draw water, out of them themselves
springs sweetest drink, and, suckling, clings a new life
to their life, and the children soon grow large.
No, I am a woman craving woman's fortune!
Far rather dead than living and not living.

She bursts into passionate weeping.

ELEKTRA

Stop howling! Go, get in! There is your place!

A whip cracks.

What's all that noise there?

(mocking her)
Could it be perhaps
they've fixed your wedding day? I hear them running,
the whole house is up. They're breeding,
or they are murdering! When there's a dearth of corpses
for their pillows, then they have to murder!

---

in kalten Nächten, wenn der Sturm die Hütte
zusammenschüttelt!
Hörst du mich an? Sprich zu mir, Schwester!

ELEKTRA

Armes Geschöpf!

CHRYSOTHEMIS

Hab Mitleid mit dir selber und mit mir!
Wem frommt denn solche Qual?
Der Vater, der ist tot. Der Bruder kommt nicht heim.
Immer sitzen wir auf der Stange
wie angehängte Vögel, wenden links
und rechts den Kopf und niemand kommt
— kein Bruder,
kein Bote von dem Bruder, nicht der Bote
[16c]von einem Boten, nichts! Mit Messern
gräbt Tag um Tag in dein und mein Gesicht
sein Mal, und draussen geht die Sonne auf
und ab, und Frauen, die ich schlank gekannt hab',
sind schwer von Segen, mühn sich zum Brunnen,
heben kaum die Eimer, und auf einmal
sind sie entbunden ihrer Last, kommen
zum Brunnen wieder und aus ihnen selber
quillt süsser Trank und säugend hängt ein Leben
[16b]an ihnen und die Kinder werden gross.
Nein, ich bin ein Weib und will ein Weiberschicksal.
Viel lieber tot, als leben und nicht leben.

ELEKTRA

Was heulst du? Fort! Hinein! Dort ist dein Platz!

Es geht ein Lärm los.

Stellen sie vielleicht
für dich die Hochzeit an? Ich hör' sie laufen.
Das ganze Haus ist auf. Sie kreissen, oder
sie morden. Wenn es an Leichen mangelt,
drauf zu schlafen, müssen sie doch morden!

CHRYSOTHEMIS

Be quick, and hide now, so that you're not [17] Geh fort, verkriech dich! Dass sie dich
seen! nicht sieht.
You must not cross her path today; she Stell' dich ihr heut' nicht in den Weg: sie
spells schickt
death with every look. She's had a [18] Tod aus jedem Blick. Sie hat geträumt.
dream.

The noise of many people hurring to and fro within gradually draws nearer.

Get out of here! They're coming through Geh fort von hier. Sie kommen durch die
the passageways. Gänge.
They're coming right past here. She's Sie kommen hier vorbei. Sie hat geträumt:
had a dream. She's had a dream, sie hat geträumt:
I don't know what. I heard about it ich weiss nicht was, ich hab' es
all from the maids. von den Mägden gehört.
They say it was about Orest, yes, Orest Sie sagen, dass sie von Orest, von Orest,
she'd dreamt of, geträumt hat,
that she had screamed out while sound dass sie geschrien hat aus ihrem Schlaf,
asleep,
as one might scream who's being choked. [19a]wie einer schreit, den man erwürgt.

Torches and people fill the passage to the left of the door. [19c]

They're coming now! She drives the maids Sie kommen schon. Sie treibt die Mägde
before her, alle
each holding up a torch. They're dragging mit Fackeln vor sich her. Sie schleppen
beasts Tiere
out, and ritual daggers. Sister, when she's und Opfermesser. Schwester, wenn sie
frightened, zittert,
she's her most horrible. ist sie am schrecklichsten.

(with urgency)

       Don't stay here now!   Geh' ihr nur heut',
Today I beg you, keep out of her way! nur diese Stunde geh' aus ihrem Weg!

ELEKTRA

I've not had such an urge for conversation Ich habe eine Lust, mit meiner Mutter
with
my mother as I have now. zu reden wie noch nie!

CHRYSOTHEMIS

      I will not listen!   Ich will's nicht hören!

She rushes off through the gate of the courtyard. A hurried procession clatters and staggers past the luridly lighted windows; it is a wrenching, a dragging of cattle, a muffled howl, a quickly choked cry, the hissing of a whip in the air, a struggling of fallen men and beasts, a staggering onwards. In the broad window appears Klytemnestra. Her sallow, bloated face appears, in the lurid glare of the torches, still paler over her scarlet robe. She is leaning on her trusted confidante, who is draped in dark violet, and on a bejewelled ivory staff. A jaundiced figure, with black hair combed back like an Egyptian woman, with a smooth face, resembling a rearing snake, carries the train of her robe. The Queen is covered over and over with gems and talismans, her arms are laden with armlets, her fingers bristle with rings. The lids of her eyes are larger than is natural, and it seems to cost her an unspeakable effort to keep them from falling. Elektra raises herself. Klytemnestra instantly opens her eyes, advances trembling with anger towards the window and points with her staff at Elektra. [17, 19c, 6, 14a, 22, 5]

KLYTEMNESTRA

What is it? See there, look! Just look [19] Was willst du? Seht doch, dort! So seht
at that! doch das!
How it rears upwards with its puffed-up Wie es sich aufbäumt mit geblähtem Hals
throat
turned to me, hissing! And that I leave und nach mir züngelt! Und das lass ich
free frei
to run about my house here! in meinem Hause laufen!

(breathing heavily)

If she could, her look would gladly kill me Wenn sie mich mit ihren Blicken töten
outright! könnte!
Great gods! Oh, why lay this weight on O Götter, warum liegt ihr so auf mir?
me?

Oh, why make wasteland out of me? Oh, [14b] | Warum verwüstet ihr mich so? Warum
why |
must all my strength in me be crippled? | muss meine Kraft in mir gelähmt sein?
Oh, why | Warum
am I a living carcass, like a desolate | [20] bin ich lebendigen Leibes wie ein wustes
field with this great nettle sprouting | Gefild und diese Nessel wächst aus mir
out of me? And I have not the strength | heraus, und ich hab' nicht die Kraft zu
to weed it! | jäten!
Why has this come to me, eternal gods? | Warum geschieht mir das, ihr ew'gen
 | Götter?

ELEKTRA
(calmly)

What gods? Are you not yourself a | [1b] Die Götter! Bist doch selber eine Göttin,
goddess |
just as they are? | bist, was sie sind!

KLYTEMNESTRA
(to her companions)

Did you both hear? D'you understand | Habt ihr gehört? Habt ihr
that, what she's saying? | verstanden, was sie redet?

CONFIDANTE

That you too | Dass auch du
are from the race of gods. | von Stamm der Götter bist.

TRAINBEARER
(hissing)

She's being spiteful. | Sie meint es tückisch.

KLYTEMNESTRA
(as her heavy eyelids droop, gently)

That sound's well-known to me. Like | Das klingt mir so bekannt. Und nur als
things I might | hätt' ich's
have forgotten long ago. She knows me | vergessen, lang und lang. Sie kennt mich
well. | gut.
But no one knows what secret thoughts | [5] Doch weiss man nie, was sie im Schilde
she hides. | [20] führt.

The Confidante and the Trainbearer whisper to each other.

ELEKTRA
(coming gradually closer to Klytemnestra) [1b, 24b]

You are yourself no longer. And those | [21] Du bist nicht mehr du selber. Das
worms | Gewürm
still hang about your hair. All that you | hängt immerfort um dich! Was sie ins
hear | Ohr
them hissing tears your senses more and | dir zischen, trennt dein Denken fort und
more | fort
in two, and that is why you go deliriously | entzwei, so gehst du hin im Taumel,
round | immer
as in a dream. | [18] bist du, als wie im Traum.

KLYTEMNESTRA

I'm going down there! [22] | Ich will hinunter.
Come! Come! I want to speak with her. [21] Lasst, lasst, ich will mit ihr reden.
She leaves the window and appears with her attendants in the doorway, and speaks from the threshold, more gently.

She exudes no | Sie ist heute
disgust today. She says things like a | nicht widerlich. Sie redet wie ein Arzt.
priest. |

CONFIDANTE
(whispering)

She doesn't say what she means. | [20] Sie redet nicht, wie sie's meint.

99

Each word she speaks is falsehood.

Ein jedes Wort ist Falschheit.

(flaring up)

I will not listen! All that you relate to me
is just the echo of Aegisth.
And when at nights I wake you, doesn't each
of you say something different? Shrieking out
that both my eyes are swollen up and bloodshot,
and that my liver's failing? And don't you then whine
in my other ear that you have seen gruesome demon
beasts, with long and pointed beaks,
suck from my veins the life-blood? Do you [20] not
point out the marks upon my flesh, and don't I take
heed and slaughter, slaughter, slaughter, [19c] victim
on victim? Won't you drive me with your [17] speeches
and contradictions to my death? I'll not
listen further: that is true and that is untrue.

Ich will nichts hören! Was aus euch herauskommt,
ist nur der Atem des Aegisth.
Und wenn ich nachts euch wecke, redet ihr
nicht jede etwas andres? Schreist nicht du,
dass meine Augenlider angeschwollen
und meine Leber krank ist? Und winselst
nicht du ins and're Ohr, dass du Dämonon
gesehen hast mit langen spitzen Schnäbeln,
die mir das Blut aussaugen? Zeigst du nicht
die Spuren mir an meinem Fleisch, und folg' ich
dir nicht und schlachte, schlachte, schlachte Opfer
um Opfer? Zerrt ihr mich mit euren Reden
und Gegenreden nicht zu Tod? Ich will nicht
mehr hören: das ist wahr und das ist Lüge.

(in a hollow voice)

Of what truth consists, no one ever can show. If she brings me tidings,

Was die Wahrheit ist, das bringt kein Mensch heraus. Wenn sie zu mir redet,

(still breathing heavily)

which please my ear to hear,
then I shall listen to what she tells me.
If someone has some pleasant thing to say,

was mich zu hören freut,
so will ich horchen, auf was sie redet.
Wenn einer etwas Angenehmes sagt,

(violently)

although it be my daughter, even her there,
I will divest my soul of all its wrappings
happily and allow the gentle breeze
to waft from where it may into me,
as the sick men do when in the evening air
they sit by water, airing all their ulcers
and suppurating wounds in the cooling
atmospheres of evening ... and think nothing other
than respite from suffering. Leave me alone with her!

und wär' es meine Tochter, wär' es die da,
will ich von meiner Seele alle Hüllen
abstreifen und das Fächeln sanfter Luft,
von wo es kommen mag, einlassen, wie
die Kranken tun, wenn sie der kühlen Luft,
am Teiche sitzend, abends ihre Beulen
und all ihr Eiterndes der kühlen Luft
preisgeben abends ... und nichts andres denken,
als Lindrung zu schaffen. [23] Lasst mich allein mit ihr!

She makes an impatient gesture with her staff, bidding the Confidante and the Trainbearer go into the building. They disappear after lingering at the door. The torches, too, disappear, and only a feeble ray of light shines from the entrance hall onto the courtyard and here and there illuminates the figures of the two women. Klytemnestra descends.

My sleep at nights is racked with torment. Have you
no remedy for my dreaming?

[24] Ich habe keine guten Nächte. Weisst du
kein Mittel gegen Träume?

Dreaming, mother? [18]

Träumst du, Mutter?

As one gets old, one dreams. But then
they can
be dispensed with. There are rituals.
There must for all things be the proper
rituals.
That's why I am so
festooned with jewels, for there lies in
each one,
for certain, special power. We need know
only
how they can each be used. If you but
wished it
you could impart some knowledge that
would help.

Wer älter wird, der träumt. Allein, es
lässt sich
vertreiben. Es gibt Bräuche.
Es muss für alles richt'ge Bräuche
geben.
Darum bin ich so
[23] behängt mit Steinen, denn es wohnt in
jedem
ganz sicher eine Kraft. Man muss nur
wissen,
wie man sie nützen kann. Wenn du nur
wolltest,
[21] du könntest etwas sagen, was mir
nützt.

ELEKTRA

I, mother, I? — Ich, Mutter, Ich?

KLYTEMNESTRA
(in a vehement outburst)

Yes, you! For you are wise.
Inside your head you have great
strength.
You could impart much knowledge that
would help.
But if a word is nothing more! What is
then
a breath? There crawls though, between
day and night,
when I lie down with open eyes, a
something,
all over me. It's not a word, it's not

a pain, it has no weight, it does not
choke.
It's nothing, certainly no ghoul, yet
somehow
it is so horrible, my soul

has only one wish: to hang itself. And
every limb
in me cries out for death, and yet I live
still.
I'm not even ill. You see me here:

do I appear unhealthy? Can one then

go on living, like a putrid carcass?
Can one disintegrate although not
ailing?
Just crumble, though quite conscious,
like a corpse
devoured by crawling maggots? And then
sleeping,
I dream, dream, dream that in my
bones
all the marrow melts, again I start
awake,
and from the water-clock not even one
tenth
has emptied, and under the curtain

Ja, du! Denn du bist klug.
In deinem Kopf ist alles stark.
Du könntest vieles sagen, was mir
nützt.
Wenn auch ein Wort nichts weiter ist!
Was ist denn
[24c] ein Hauch? Und doch kriecht zwischen
Tag und Nacht,
wenn ich mit offnen Augen lieg', ein
Etwas
hin über mich. Es ist kein Wort, es
ist
kein Schmerz, es drückt mich nicht, es
würgt mich nicht.
[24b] Nichts ist es, nicht einmal ein Alp, und
dennoch,
es ist so fürchterlich, dass meine
Seele
sich wünscht, erhängt zu sein, und jedes
Glied
in mir schreit nach dem Tod, und dabei
leb' ich
und bin nicht einmal krank: du siehst
mich doch:
seh' ich wie eine Kranke? Kann man
denn
vergehn, lebend, wie ein faules Aas?
Kann man zerfallen, wenn man gar nicht
krank ist?
[24a] Zerfallen wachen Sinnes, wie ein
Kleid,
zerfressen von den Motten? Und dann
schlaf' ich
und träume, träume, dass sich mir das
Mark
in den Knocken löst, und taumle wieder
auf,
und nicht der zehnte Teil der
Wasseruhr
ist abgelaufen, und was unterm
Vorhang

what grins there is not yet the sallow
  morning,
no, always it's the torch beside the
  door
that winks at me, just like a living
  monster
on my sleep espying.
These dreams must have a
conclusion . . . something . . . whosoever
  sends them,
each evil demon leaves us be, as soon
What sort of offering? And at what hour?
  And where?

hereingrinst, ist noch nicht der fahle
  Morgen,
nein, immer noch die Fackel vor der
  Tür,
die grässlich zuckt, wie ein Lebendiges
[24c]und meinem Schlaf belauert.
Diese Träume müssen
ein Ende haben. Wer sie immer
  schickt,
ein jeder Dämon lässt von uns,
  sobald
das rechte Blut geflossen ist.

ELEKTRA

All demons!   Ein jeder!

KLYTEMNESTRA
(*wildly*)

And if I take each beast that crawls and
  flies
and bleed its veins dry, and in bloody
  vapours
wake up and go to sleep like the
  people
of distant Thule in their red bloody
  nimbus:
I'll stop this awful dreaming.

Und müsst ich jedes Tier, das kriecht
  und fliegt,
[19c]zur Ader lassen und im Dampf des
  Blutes
aufsteh'n und schlafen gehn wie die
  Völker
des letzten Thule in blutroten Nebel:

ich will nicht länger träumen.

ELEKTRA

When the right   Wenn das rechte
blood sacrifice beneath the hatchet falls, [24a]Blutopfer unterm Beile fällt, dann
  your   träumst du
dreaming will finish!   nicht länger!

KLYTEMNESTRA
(*very hastily*)

So do you then know with which   Also wüsstest du mit welchem
of the ordained beasts?   geweihten Tier? —

ELEKTRA
(*with a mysterious smile*)

With one that's not ordained yet.   Mit einem ungeweihten!

KLYTEMNESTRA

That's lying bound within?   Das drin gebunden liegt?

ELEKTRA

No, it runs free.   Nein! Es läuft frei.

KLYTEMNESTRA

What are the rituals?   Und was für Bräuche?

ELEKTRA

Wonderful rituals,   Wunderbare Bräuche,
enacted very strictly.   und sehr genau zu üben.

KLYTEMNESTRA
(*vehemently*)

Tell me then!   Rede doch!

ELEKTRA

Can you not guess my meaning?   Kannst du mich nicht erraten?

KLYTEMNESTRA

No, so I'm asking.

(as if solemnly adjuring Elektra)

Come, name the sacrificial beast!

Nein, darum frag' ich.

[24c]Den Namen sag' des Opfertiers!

ELEKTRA

A woman. [23]

Ein Weib.

KLYTEMNESTRA

Could it be one of my own serving maids?
A child? A young virgin perhaps? A woman
known by man already?

Von meinen Dienerinnen eine, sag'!
Ein Kind? Ein jungfräuliches Weib? Ein Weib,
das schon erkannt vom Manne?

ELEKTRA
(calmly)

Yes, she's known,
that's right!

Ja! Erkannt!
Das ist's!

KLYTEMNESTRA
(pressing her for an answer)

What sort of offering? And at what hour? And where?

Und wie das Opfer? Und welche Stunde? Und wo?

ELEKTRA
(calm)

At any place, at any hour
of day and of night.

An jedem Ort, zu jeder Stunde
des Tags und der Nacht.

KLYTEMNESTRA

The ritual, say!
How is it done? I must myself . . .

Die Bräuche sag'!
Wie brächt ich's dar? Ich selber muss . . .

ELEKTRA

No, this time
you won't go on the hunt with net and with axe.

Nein. Diesmal
gehst du nicht auf die Jagd mit Netz und mit Beil.

KLYTEMNESTRA

Who then? Who does the rite?

Wer denn? Wer brächt es dar?

ELEKTRA

A man.

Ein Mann.

KLYTEMNESTRA

Aegisth?

Aegisth?

ELEKTRA
(laughing)

Did I not say a man?

Ich sagte doch: ein Mann!

KLYTEMNESTRA

Who? Give me answer!
A man from this house? Or a stranger brought from
outside?

Wer? Gib mir Antwort.
[18] Vom Hause jemand? Oder muss ein Fremder
herbei?

ELEKTRA
(staring absently at the ground)

Yes, yes, a stranger. But for certain
he comes from here.

Ja, ja, ein Fremder. Aber freilich
ist er vom Haus.

KLYTEMNESTRA

Don't set me riddles now.
Elektra, hear my words. I'm very pleased
that just for once you've lost your stubborn
manner.

Gib mir nicht Rätsel auf.
Elektra, hör' mich an. Ich freue mich,
dass ich dich heut' einmal nicht störrisch
finde.

ELEKTRA
(*softly*)

Won't you allow our brother home here,
mother?

Lässt du den Bruder nicht nach Hause,
Mutter?

KLYTEMNESTRA

I have forbidden that his name be
mentioned.

Von ihm zu reden hab' ich dir verboten.

ELEKTRA

Are you afraid of him?

So hast du Furcht vor ihm?

KLYTEMNESTRA

Who says so?

Wer sagt das?

ELEKTRA

Mother,
you're trembling!

Mutter,
du zitterst ja!

KLYTEMNESTRA

Who need have fear
of such a weak simpleton?

Wer fürchtet sich
vor einem Schwachsinnigen.

ELEKTRA

What?

Wie?

KLYTEMNESTRA

It's said he stammers,
lies outside beside the dogs and can't
differentiate man from mongrel.

Es heisst,
er stammelt, liegt im Hofe bei den Hunden
und weiss nicht Mensch und Tier zu
unterscheiden.

ELEKTRA

The child was in good health.

Das Kind war ganz gesund.

KLYTEMNESTRA

It's said they gave him
a wretched dwelling with beasts from the
yard
as his companions.

Es heisst, sie gaben
ihm schlechte Wohnung und Tiere

des Hofes zur Gesellschaft.

ELEKTRA

Ah!

Ah!

KLYTEMNESTRA
(*with drooping eyelids*)

I sent off
much gold and yet more gold that he
should be
well-treated, like a child of kings.

Ich schickte
viel Gold und wieder Gold, sie sollten ihn

gut halten wie ein Königskind.

ELEKTRA

You lie!
You sent off gold whereby he might be
strangled.

Du lügst!
Du schicktest Gold, damit sie ihn
erwürgen.

Who told you that?   We sagt dir das?

      I see it in your eyes now, [18]   Ich seh's an deinen Augen.
but merely from your trembling I can   Allein an deinem Zittern seh' ich auch,
  see
that he still lives, that you by day and   dass er noch lebt. Dass du bei Tag und
  night   Nacht
think no thought but of him, and that   [25a]an nichts denkst als an ihn. Dass dir das
  your heart   Herz
dries up with terror, for you know: he'll   verdorrt vor Grauen, weil du weisst: er
  come.   kommt.

Why should I care who is outside there?   Was kümmert mich, wer ausser Haus ist.
I live in here and am the mistress. I've   [14a]Ich lebe hier und bin die Herrin. Diener
  servants
here enough to fortify each doorway,   hab' ich genug, die Tore zu bewachen,
and if I wish both day and night   und wenn ich will, lass ich bei Tag und
                                                                  Nacht
I'll place outside my chamber three   vor meiner Kammer drei Bewaffnete
  armed men
with eyes wide open, alert to danger. And   mit offenen Augen sitzen. Und aus dir
  from you
I shall somehow or other bring to light   bring' ich so oder so das rechte Wort
that single word. Already you've let slip   schon an den Tag. Du hast dich schon
                                                                  verraten,
that you know the fitting sacrifice and   dass du das rechte Opfer weisst und auch
proper rites which can assist me. If you're   die Bräuche, die mir nützen. Sagst du's
  mute   nicht
in freedom, with the help of chains you'll   [14a, b] im Freien, wirst du's an der Kette sagen.
If mute when fed, you'll talk when hungry.   Sagst du's nicht satt, so sagst du's
  Dreams   hungernd. Träume
are just something to be rid of. He who   sind etwas, das man los wird. Wer dran
  suffers   leidet
and doesn't find the means to cure   und nicht das Mittel findet, sich zu
  himself   heilen,
is merely a fool. I shall find out myself   ist nur ein Narr. Ich finde mir heraus,
whose blood must run and then I'll sleep   wer bluten muss, damit ich wieder schlafe.
  so soundly.

(leaping out of the dark at Klytemnestra, coming nearer and nearer to her, growing more and more terrifying)

What blood must run? Your own, from   Was bluten muss? Dein eigenes Genick,
  your own neck,
when for the kill the hunter captures   wenn dich der Jäger abgefangen hat!
  you!
I hear him go from room to room, I hear   Ich hör' ihn durch die Zimmer gehn, ich
  how   hör' ihn
he raises up the bedside curtain: who'd   [25a]den Vorhang von dem Bette heben: wer
  slaughter   schlachtet
a victim in his sleep? He hunts you up;   ein Opfertier im Schlaf? Er jagt dich auf,
screaming you flee away. Ah, but he, he   schreiend entfliehst du, aber er, er ist
  is right behind,   hinterdrein:
he drives you through the house! First to   er treibt dich durch das Haus! Willst du
  the right,   nach rechts,
there is the bed! Then left, there foams   da steht das Bett! Nach links, da schäumt
  the bath   das Bad
like blood! The darkness and the torches   wie Blut! Das Dunkel und die Fackeln
  cast   werfen
their black-purple nets of death all over   schwarzrote Todesnetze über dich.
  you.

Klytemnestra, shaking, speechless with terror, turns towards the palace. Elektra, seizing her robe, drags her forward. Klytemnestra retreats towards the wall. Her eyes gape with terror. Her staff falls from her trembling hands.

Then down the stairway, through the cellar there,	Hinab die Treppen durch Gewölbe hin,
through cellar after cellar goes the hunt —	Gewölbe und Gewölbe geht die Jagd —
and I, I, I, I who sent him to you,	[25b]Und ich! Ich! Ich, die ihn dir geschickt,
I'll be like a hound snapping at your heels.	ich bin wie ein Hund an deiner Ferse,
And were you to find a hole, I'd spring out	willst du in eine Höhle, spring' ich dich
at you sideways on. And so we'll drive you on	von seitwärts an. So treiben wir dich fort,
until a wall shuts off the way, and there,	bis eine Mauer alles sperrt und dort
in deepest darkness, yes, I see him well,	im tiefsten Dunkel, doch ich seh' ihn wohl,
a shadow, and yet limbs and the white	[9] ein Schatten und doch Glieder und das Weisse
of an eye are visible, there sits my father.	von einem Auge doch, da sitzt der Vater:
He pays no heed, and yet it must be done.	er achtet's nicht und doch muss es geschehn:
So at his feet we throw you to the ground.	zu seinen Füssen drücken wir dich hin.
You'd like to cry out, but the stifling air	Du möchtest schreien, doch die Luft erwürgt
snuffs out the unborn cry and leaves it silent	den ungebornen Schrei und lässt ihn lautlos
to fall to earth. As if crazy, offering	[22] zu Boden fallen. Wie von Sinnen häust du
up your neck you feel the keen sharpness	den Nacken hin, fühlst schon die Schärfe zucken
quivering at the seat of life. Yet he holds	bis an den Sitz des Lebens. Doch er hält
the blow in check, the rituals are not yet fulfilled.	den Schlag zurück: die Bräuche sind noch nicht erfüllt.
All is still; you only hear your heart	Alles schweigt, du hörst dein eignes Herz
against your ribs pulsating. All this time —	an deinen Rippen schlagen: diese Zeit —
it stretches before you like a dark abyss	sie dehnt sich vor dir wie ein finstrer Schlund
of ages — all this time is given to you	von Jahren. — Diese Zeit ist dir gegeben
to imagine how the shipwrecked sailors' spirits	zu ahnen, wie es Scheiternden zumute ist,
are when their wild ineffective cries dissolve	wenn ihr vergebliches Geschrei die Schwärze
in the blackness of the clouds and of death.	der Wolken und des Todes zerfrisst, diese Zeit
All this time is given to you to envy all those people	ist dir gegeben, alle zu beneiden,
who, fettered fast to walls of darkest dungeons,	die angeschmiedet sind an Kerkermauern,
who, from the depths of wells, cry out for death	die auf dem Grund von Brunnen nach dem Tod
to grant them a quick deliverance. For you,	als wie nach Erlösung schrei'n — denn du,
you lie within yourself so fast imprisoned,	du liegst in deinem Selbst so eingekerkert,
as in the red-hot bowels of some great beast	als wär's der glühnde Bauch von einem Tier
of brass and, just as now, you cannot cry out!	von Erz — und so wie jetzt kannst du nicht schrein!
Before you	Da steh' ich
I'll stand and you'll read with your staring eyes	vor dir, und nun liest du mit starrem Aug'

Edith Coates as Klytemnestra at Covent Garden in 1953 (Royal Opera House Archives)

the abominable word that clearly on my face	das ungeheure Wort, das mir in mein Gesicht geschrieben ist:
is chiselled out:	
you've hanged your very spirit in a noose	erhängt ist dir die Seele in der selbst-
of your own knotting. Whistling falls the [13]	gedrehten Schlinge, sausend fällt das Beil,
axe,	
and I stand there. At last I watch you [25b]	und ich steh' da und seh' dich endlich
dying.	sterben!
Your dreams will then stop. I'll have no further need	Dann träumst du nicht mehr, dann brauche ich
for dreaming, and all who live on	nicht mehr zu träumen, und wer dann noch lebt,
exult, and celebrate a life of joy!	der jauchzt und kann sich seines Lebens freun!

They stand eye to eye — Elektra in wild intoxication, Klytemnestra breathing in horrible spasms of fear. At this moment the interior of the entrance hall is lighted up. The Confidante comes running out. She whispers something into Klytemnestra's ear. She seems at first not to understand. Gradually she grasps the meaning of it all. She commands lights. Serving maids come running with torches and range themselves behind Klytemnestra. Klytemnestra commands more lights. The Trainbearer appears. Still more serving maids come running out and range themselves behind Klytemnestra so that the courtyard is flooded with light and a reddish yellow glare eddies round the walls. Now her features gradually change and the tension yields to a look of evil triumph. Klytemnestra causes the message to be whispered to her again; meanwhile she does not take her eyes off Elektra for an instant. Glutted with wild joy, Klytemnestra raises both her hands, threateningly, towards Elektra. Then the Confidante picks her staff up from the ground and, leaning on both, Klytemnestra hurries eagerly into the palace, gathering up her robe on the stairs. The serving maids rush after her with the torches, as if pursued. [25a, b]

What did they say to her? She's overjoyed.	Was sagen sie ihr denn? Sie freut sich ja!
My head! I cannot think! Why is the woman	Mein Kopf! Mir fällt nichts ein! Worüber freut sich
so pleased?	das Weib?

Chrysothemis runs through the courtyard gate, howling like a wounded beast.

CHRYSOTHEMIS
(screaming)

Orest! Orest is dead! [27a]	Orest! Orest ist tot!

ELEKTRA
(making a gesture to ward her off, as if demented)

Be quiet!	Sei still!

CHRYSOTHEMIS

Orest is dead![32b]	Orest ist tot!

Elektra moves her lips.

I came outside; already they knew! They were	Ich kam hinaus, da wussten sie's schon! Alle
standing around and everyone knew apart	standen herum und alle wussten es schon,
from us two.	nur wir nicht.

ELEKTRA

No one knows it.	Niemand weiss es.

CHRYSOTHEMIS

All know it.	Alle wissen's!

ELEKTRA

No one can know it, for it isn't true.	Niemand kann's wissen: denn es is nicht wahr.

Chrysothemis flings herself on the ground in despair. Elektra drags her up. [32b, 24]

It is not true! It is not true! I say to you,	Es ist nicht wahr! Es ist nicht wahr! Ich sag' dir doch,
it is not true!	es ist nicht wahr!

CHRYSOTHEMIS

The strangers stood by the wall, the strangers
who knew and were sent to inform us two,
an old man and a young one. They already had
told them all; around them both stood everyone
in a crowd, and all knew, all knew.
(with a supreme effort)
All had been told.

Die Fremden standen an der Wand, die Fremden,
die hergeschickt sind, es zu melden: zwei,
ein Alter und ein Junger. Allen hatten
sie's schon erzählt, im Kreise standen alle
um sie herum und alle,
alle wussten es schon.

ELEKTRA
(with all her strength)

It is not true!

[1] Es ist nicht wahr!

CHRYSOTHEMIS

But we don't matter. Dead, Elektra, dead!
Departed in a strange land! Dead!
Departed far away from here.
By his own horses struck senseless and dragged off.

An uns denkt niemand. Tot! Elektra, tot!
Gestorben in der Fremde! Tot!
Gestorben dort in fremden Land,
Von seinen Pferden erschlagen und geschleift.

In wild despair she sinks to the ground by Elektra's side, near the threshold. A young servant comes hurriedly out of the building, and stumbles over the woman lying by the threshold.

YOUNG SERVANT

Mind out! Who loafs like that beside a [28] door?
Ah, I might have guessed it! Hey there, stablelad, hey!

Platz da! Wer lungert so vor einer Tür?
Ah! Konnt' mir's denken! Heda, Stallung! He!

OLD SERVANT
(appearing at the courtyard gate, scowling)

What's needed there?

Was soll's im Stall?

YOUNG SERVANT

A mount must be saddled, and at lightning speed, d'you hear me?
A nag, a donkey, or as far as I'm concerned,
get a cow, but fast!

Gesattelt soll werden, und so rasch als möglich!
Hörst du?
Ein Gaul, ein Maultier oder meinetwegen
auch eine Kuh, nur rasch!

OLD SERVANT

For whom?

Für wen?

YOUNG SERVANT

For him who gives you command. He gapes there! Quick, for me!
At once for me! Move, move! I must go out now
to the fields, the master's out there, and I've a
message he must be given, such a message,
urgent enough to ride one of your hacks
to a death pre-empted.

Für den, der's dir befiehlt. Da glotzt er! Rasch, für mich!
Sofort! Für mich! Trab, trab! Weil ich hinaus muss
aufs Feld, den Herren holen, weil ich ihm
Botschaft zu bringen habe, grosse Botschaft,
wichtig genug, um eine eurer Mähren
zu Tod zu reiten.

Exeunt Young and Old Servants.

ELEKTRA
(to herself, softly, but with determination)

Now it is left for us to do.　　　　　　　　[29] Nun muss es hier von uns geschehn.

CHRYSOTHEMIS
(astonished, questioning)

　　　　　Elektra?　　　　　　　　　　　　　　　　　　　Elektra?

ELEKTRA
(in frenzied haste)

　　　　　　　We,　　　　　　　　　　　　　　　　　　　　Wir!
we two must do the deed.　　　　　　　Wir beide müssen's tun.

CHRYSOTHEMIS

　　　What, Elektra?　　　　　　　　　　　　Was, Elektra?

ELEKTRA
(softly)

At best today, at best this very night.　　Am besten heut', am besten diese Nacht.

CHRYSOTHEMIS

What, sister?　　　　　　　　　　　　Was, Schwester?

ELEKTRA
(very sadly)

　　　What? The task that now befalls　　　Was? Das Werk, das nun auf uns
the two of us, as he now cannot come.　[32] gefallen ist, weil er nicht kommen kann.

CHRYSOTHEMIS
(in growing fear)

What sort of task?　　　　　　　　　Was für ein Werk?

ELEKTRA

　　　　We have to, you and I,　　　　　　　Nun müssen du und ich
go there to that slut and to her man,　　hingehn und das Weib und ihren Mann
and kill them.　　　　　　　　　　[29] erschlagen.

CHRYSOTHEMIS
(with a slight shudder)

　　Sister, do you mean our mother?　　　Schwester, sprichst du von der Mutter?

ELEKTRA
(wildly)

Yes, her and also him. It must be done　　Von ihr. Und auch von ihm. Ganz ohne
　with no more　　　　　　　　　　　　Zögern
delay. Keep quiet. There's nothing to　　muss es geschehn. Schweig still. Zu
　say,　　　　　　　　　　　　　　　　sprechen ist nichts.
nor even to consider, except: how?　　　Nichts gibt es zu bedenken, als nur: wie?
How we will do it?　　　　　　　　　Wie wir es tun.

CHRYSOTHEMIS

　　　　I?　　　　　　　　　　　　　　　Ich?

ELEKTRA

　　Yes, you and I. Who else?　　　　　　Ja. Du und ich. Wer sonst?

CHRYSOTHEMIS
(horrified)

We, we two should go inside there? We,　　Wir? Wir beide sollen hingehn? Wir? Wir
　we two　　　　　　　　　　　　　　　zwei
should go with our bare hands there?　　mit unsern beiden Händen?

ELEKTRA

　　　　Don't be concerned.　　　　　　　　　　　Dafür lass
I shall plan it.　　　　　　　　　　du mich nur sorgen.
(mysteriously)
The axe,　　　　　　　　　　　　Das Beil!
(more loudly)
　the axe with which our father … [13]　　Das Beil, womit der Vater —

110

CHRYSOTHEMIS

You? How horrible, you have it? Du? Entsetzliche, du hast es?

ELEKTRA

For our brother   Für den Bruder
I guarded it. Now it is for us to wield it.   bewahrt' ich es. Nun müssen wir es
                                   schwingen.

CHRYSOTHEMIS

You? Do you ask these arms to strike   Du? Diese Arme den Aegisth erschlagen?
Aegisth dead?

ELEKTRA
(wildly)

First her, then him. First him, then her.   Erst sie, dann ihn; erst ihn, dann sie,
Either.   gleichviel.

CHRYSOTHEMIS

I'm terrified!   Ich fürchte mich.

ELEKTRA

There's no one sleeping in their   Es schläft niemand in ihrem Vorgemach.
anteroom.

CHRYSOTHEMIS

Asleep you'd kill them!   Im Schlaf sie morden!

ELEKTRA

Asleep they're simply tethered victims.   Wer schläft, ist ein gebundnes Opfer.
 If they   Schliefen
had slept apart I could alone complete   sie nicht zusamm', könnt' ich's allein
it.   vollbringen.
So you must come as well.   So aber musst du mit.

CHRYSOTHEMIS
(resisting)

Elektra!   Elektra!

ELEKTRA

You, you!   Du! Du!
For you are strong.   Denn du bist stark!
(standing close to Chrysothemis)
How strong you are! The nights [31]   Wie stark du bist! Dich haben
spent in fresh virginal sleep have made you   die jungfräulichen Nächte stark gemacht.
 strong.
Everywhere you have such strength in   Überall ist so viel Kraft in dir!
 you!
You have sinews like a filly,   Sehnen hast du wie ein Füllen,
and your feet are slender.   schlank sind deine Füsse.
How slim and supple —   Wie schlank und biegsam —
I can wind round you —   leicht umschling ich sie, —
are your haunches made!   deine Hüften sind!
You'd worm your way through any cleft,   Du windest dich durch jeden Spalt, du
 you'd get through   hebst dich
a window! Let me have your arms to feel   durchs Fenster! Lass mich deine Arme
 them,   fühlen!
how cool and strong they are. As you resist   wie kühl und stark sie sind! Wie du mich
 me   abwehrst,
I feel what arms they really are! You'd   fühl' ich, was das für Arme sind. Du
 easily   könntest
smother what you'd chosen to. You could   erdrücken, was du an dich ziehst. Du
 take   könntest
me, or indeed a man, within your arms and   mich, oder einen Mann in deinen Armen
 then choke him.   ersticken!
Everywhere you have such strength in   Überall ist so viel Kraft in dir!
 you!
It flows like cool and   Sie strömt wie kühles,
refreshing water from a rock. It streams   verhaltnes Wasser aus dem Fels. Sie flutet
 down

111

just as your hair does, on your powerful
shoulders below!
I feel through the coolness of your skin
the warm red blood pulsate, and with my
cheek
I feel the soft down upon your youthful
body.
You are full of strength, you are fair,
you are just like a fruit on its ripest day.

mit deinen Haaren auf die starken
Schultern herab!
Ich spüre durch die Kühle deiner Haut
das warme Blut hindurch, mit meiner
Wange
spür' ich den Flaum auf deinen jungen
Armen.
Du bist voller Kraft, du bist schön,
du bist wie eine Frucht an der Reife Tag.

CHRYSOTHEMIS

Leave me!

Lass mich!

ELEKTRA

No, I'll hold you close!
With my poor melancholy withered arms [32a]
entwined about your frame, as you resist

you will just pull the draw-strings even
tighter.
All around you I'll wind myself, I'll sink
down deep my taproots in you; I'll implant
my strength
of will deep in your blood.

Nein, ich halte dich!
Mit meinen traurigen verdorrten Armen
umschling ich deinen Leib, wie du dich
sträubst,
ziehst du den Knoten nur noch fester,
ranke
will ich mich rings um dich, versenken
meine Wurzeln in dich und mit meinem
Willen
[39b]dir impfen das Blut!

CHRYSOTHEMIS

Let me go!

Lass mich!

She retreats a few steps.

ELEKTRA

(hurrying wildly after her and seizing her robe)

No, I'll not let go!

Nein! Ich lass dich nicht!

CHRYSOTHEMIS

Elektra, hear me!
You are so wise, help us get out of here!
Help us to freedom! Elektra, help us, help
us to freedom!

Elektra, hör' mich.
Du bist so klug, hilf uns aus diesem Haus,
hilf uns ins Freie. Elektra, hilf uns, hilf uns
ins Freie!

ELEKTRA

I'll be a proper sister from now on, [10]
a sister such as I have never been!
I'll sit down with you in your room
attending loyally,
and wait there for your bridegroom. For
him
I shall anoint you, and you'll plunge in a
bath
sweetly fragrant just like a youthful
swan.
And on my breast I'll hide your modest
blushes,
till he takes you, who through your veil are
glowing
like a torch, towards the wedding couch
within his powerful arms.

Von jetzt an will ich deine Schwester sein,
so wie ich niemals deine Schwester war!
Getreu will ich mit dir in deiner Kammer
sitzen
und warten auf den Bräutigam. Für ihn
will ich dich salben und ins duftige Bad
sollst du mir tauchen wie der junge Schwan
und deinen Kopf an meiner Brust
verbergen,
bevor er dich, die durch die Schleier glüht
wie eine Fackel, in das Hochzeitsbett
mit starken Armen zieht.

CHRYSOTHEMIS

(closing her eyes)

No, sister, no.
Don't speak such words as those inside
this house.

Nicht, Schwester, nicht.
Sprich nicht ein solches Wort in diesem
Haus.

ELEKTRA

Oh, yes! More than a sister I shall be
to you
from this day on. I'll serve you

O ja! Weit mehr als Schwester bin ich dir
von diesem Tage an: ich diene dir

like a little slave girl! When you lie in labour
I'll sit there at your bedside day and night,
keeping the flies off, drawing cool fresh water.
When all at once there on your naked lap
a living object reclines, almost frighteningly
I'll lift it up high, so high that his
sweet smile from high above you will descend
to the secret deep recesses of your soul.
And there the final icy horror melts
before this sunny smile. And you with shining
tears can cry out your joy.

[2c] wie deine Sklavin. Wenn du liegst in Weh'n,
sitz ich an deinem Bette Tag und Nacht,
wehr' dir die Fliegen, schöpfe kühles Wasser,
[16a]und wenn auf einmal auf dem nackten Schoss
dir ein Lebendiges liegt, erschreckend fast,
so heb' ich's empor, so hoch, damit
sein Lächeln hoch von oben in die tiefsten,
geheimsten Klüften deiner Seele fällt
und dort das letzte, eisig Grässliche
vor dieser Sonne schmilzt und du's in hellen
Tränen ausweinen kannst.

CHRYSOTHEMIS
Oh, take me out! I'm dying in this house!

O bring' mich fort! Ich sterb' in diesem Haus!

ELEKTRA
(at Chrysothemis' knees)
Your mouth is fair;
yes, even open wide to speak in anger.
From your unsullied, powerful mouth so awesome
a cry must spurt forth, awesome like the cry
of death's great goddess, when one lies here
at your feet as I do now.

Dein Mund ist schön,
wenn er sich einmal auftut, um zu zürnen!
Aus deinen reinen, starken Mund muss furchtbar
[9] ein Schrei hervorsprüh'n, furchtbar, wie der Schrei
der Todesgöttin, wenn man unter dir
so daliegt, wie nun ich.

CHRYSOTHEMIS
What do you mean?

Was redest du?

ELEKTRA
(rising)
Before you can escape this
house and me, it must be done!

Denn eh' du diesem Haus
[24b]und mir erntkommst, musst du es tun!

Chrysothemis tries to speak. Elektra places her hand over Chrysothemis' mouth.
No other way will lead you out. I'll stay with you
till you swear, mouth to mouth with me, assurance
that you will do it.

Dir führt kein Weg hinaus als der. Ich lass dich nicht,
eh du mir Mund auf Mund es zugeschworen,
dass du es tun wirst.

CHRYSOTHEMIS
(freeing herself)
Leave me!

Lass mich!

ELEKTRA
(seizing her again)
Swear you'll come
tonight, when all is quiet, to the foot
of the stairway!

Schwör', du kommst
heut Nacht, wenn alles still ist, an den Fuss
der Treppe!

CHRYSOTHEMIS
Leave me!

Lass mich!

ELEKTRA
(clinging to her dress)
Do not struggle, girl!
Not one small drop of blood will stay upon you.

Mädchen, sträub' dich nicht!
Es bleibt kein Tropfen Blut am Leibe haften.

Quickly you'll slip the blood-stained
  garment
off and, clean of body, don nuptial
  clothes.

Schnell schlüpfst du aus dem blutigen
  Gewand
mit reinem Leib ins hochzeitliche Hemd.

CHRYSOTHEMIS
Let me go!   Lass mich!

ELEKTRA
(with still greater urgency)
Don't be a coward! Every shudder   Sei nicht zu feige! Was du jetzt
conquered now will be repaid with   an Schaudern überwindest, wird vergolten
  shudders
of ecstasy for night on night.   [16b]mit wonneschaudern Nacht für Nacht —

CHRYSOTHEMIS
I cannot!   Ich kann nicht!

ELEKTRA
Say you will come with me!   Sag, dass du kommen wirst!

CHRYSOTHEMIS
I cannot!   Ich kann nicht!

ELEKTRA
                  See,   Sieh,
I lie before you kissing your two feet.   ich lieg' vor dir, ich küsse deine Füsse!

CHRYSOTHEMIS
I cannot!   Ich kann nicht!

She rushes out by the door.

ELEKTRA
So, be damned!   Sei verflucht!
(with wild determination)
              Well then, alone!   Nun denn, allein!
*She begins to dig by the wall of the palace, at the side of the threshold, eagerly, without a sound, like an
animal. Elektra pauses in her digging, looks round, and continues. She looks round again and listens,
then digs again. Orestes stands by the gate of the courtyard, in black relief against the last rays of the
sun. He enters the courtyard. [33a] Elektra looks up at him; he turns slowly so that his eyes rest on her.
Elektra starts up violently. Trembling:*
Strange man, what brings you here? What   Was willst du, fremder Mensch? Was
  forces you   treibst du dich
to wander here at this dark hour espying   zur dunken Stunde hier herum, belauerst,
  what others do?   was andre tun!
I've business to do here. What's that to   Ich hab' hier ein Geschäft. Was kümmert's
  you?   dich?
Leave me in peace!   Lass mich in Ruh'.

ORESTES
I have to wait here.   [34] Ich muss hier warten.

ELEKTRA
              Wait here?   [36b]   Warten?

ORESTES
                  But you   Doch du bist
belong to the house? Are you a serving   hier aus dem Haus? Bist eine von den
  maid   Mägden
inside this household?   dieses Hauses?

ELEKTRA
          Yes, I serve here in the house.[33b]   Ja, ich diene hier im Haus.
You, however, have nothing to gain here.   Du aber hast hier nichts zu schaffen.
  Enjoy life,   Freu dich
and go!   und geh.

ORESTES
        I said to you, I have to wait here,   Ich sagte dir, ich muss hier warten,
until they call me.   bis sie mich rufen.

Those inside there?
You lie. I know for sure the master's not
  at home.
And she, what would she want with
  you?

Die da drinnen?
Du lügst. Weiss ich doch gut, der Herr
  ist nicht zu Haus'.
Und sie, was sollte sie mit dir?

ORESTES

I, and one other
who is with me, we bring with us a
  message
for the Queen.
    We're sent to talk to her,
as we bear testimony that her son
Orest has met his death. We saw it
  happen,
for he was dragged to death by his own
  horses.
I was as old as he, and his companion
by day and night.

Ich und noch einer,
der mit mir ist, wir haben einen Auftrag
an die Frau.
    Wir sind an sie geschickt,
weil wir bezeugen können, dass ihr Sohn
[35] Orest gestorben ist vor unsern Augen.

Denn ihn erschlugen seine eignen Pferde.

Ich war so alt wie er, und sein Gefährte
bei Tag und Nacht.

ELEKTRA

    Must I see you
here still? Why do you creep around
in my disconsolate corner,
herald of sorrow? Can't you trumpet
  forth
your dismal message there where they'll
  be glad?
Your eye stares into mine, and his is
  jelly.
Your mouth still shuts and opens; his is
clogged with earth and cannot move.
You live, and he, though better far than
  you,
your peer a thousand times, a thousand
  times more crucial
that he lives still, he is dead!

    Muss ich dich
noch sehn? Schleppst du dich hierher,
in meinen traurigen Winkel,
Herold des Unglücks! Kannst du nicht die
  Botschaft
austrompeten dort, wo sie sich freu'n!

Dein Aug' da starrt mich an, und seins ist
  Gallert.
Dein Mund geht auf und zu und seiner ist
mit Erde vollgepfropft.
Du lebst und er, der besser war als du,

und edler, tausendmal und tausendmal so
  wichtig,
dass er lebte, er ist hin.

ORESTES
(calmly)

Leave Orest in peace. He spent a life of
far too much enjoyment. The gods
  above
cannot tolerate the all-too-ringing sound
of joy. And so he had to perish.

Lass den Orest. Er freute sich zu sehr
an seinem Leben. Die Götter droben

vertragen nicht den allzu hellen Laut
der Lust. So musste er denn sterben.

ELEKTRA

But I! But I! I lie here in
the knowledge that the child cannot
  return,
cannot return.
That the child is down there in a
  gloomy
abyss of horror, that they live on inside
there still rejoicing,
that this foul brood lives out its hollow
  life,
and eats and drinks and sleeps
while I above live as no wild beast would
  ever live,
on my own and shunned. I am up here
  alone.

[10] Doch ich! Doch ich! Da liegen und
zu wissen, dass das Kind nie wieder
  kommt,
nie wieder kommt,
dass das Kind da drunten in den Klüften

das Grausens lungert, dass die da drinnen
leben und sich freuen,
dass dies Gezücht in seiner Höhle lebt

und isst und trinkt und schläft —
und ich hier droben, wie nicht das Tier des
  Waldes
einsam und grässlich lebt — ich hier
  droben allein.

ORESTES

Who are you then?

Wer bist denn du?

115

ELEKTRA

What's that to you, who I am?   Was kümmert's dich, wer ich bin?

ORESTES

Your blood must be akin to those two   Du musst verwandtes Blut zu denen sein
who have perished, Agamemnon and   die starben, Agamemnon und Orest.
Orest.

ELEKTRA

Akin? I am that blood! I am the blood   Verwandt? Ich bin dies Blut! Ich bin das
                                                                         hündisch
so brutishly shed of King Agamemnon!   vergossene Blut des Königs Agamemnon!
Elektra's my name!   Elektra heiss' ich.

ORESTES

No!   Nein!

ELEKTRA

He disagrees.   Er leugnet's ab.
He scoffs at me and takes away my name   Er bläst auf mich und nimmt mir meinen
too.   Namen.

ORESTES

Elektra!   [36b]Elektra!

ELEKTRA

As I've no father now —   Weil ich nicht Vater hab',

ORESTES

Elektra!   Elektra!

ELEKTRA

— nor brother, I am the sport of   — noch Bruder, bin ich der Spott der
rascals!   Buben!

ORESTES

Elektra! Elektra!   Elektra! Elektra!
So you are she? I really see her, you?   So seh' ich sie? Ich seh' sie wirklich? Du?
So they have let you waste with hunger!   So haben sie dich darben lassen oder —
Have they perhaps dared to beat you?   sie haben dich geschlagen?

ELEKTRA

Leave my dress! Don't pierce me with   [32a]Lass mein Kleid! Wühl nicht mit deinem
your curious look.   Blick daran.

ORESTES

Whatever have they done with all your   [37b]Was haben sie gemacht mit deinen
nights?   Nächten?
How terrible your eyes are!   Furchtbar sind deine Augen.

ELEKTRA

Leave me!   Lass mich!

ORESTES

How your cheeks are sunken!   Hohl sind deine Wangen!

ELEKTRA

Go in the house!   Geh' ins Haus,
There I have got a sister who is saving   drin hab' ich eine Schwester, die bewahrt
herself   sich
for joyous feasts!   für Freudenfeste auf!

ORESTES

Elektra, hear me!   Elektra, hör mich!

ELEKTRA

I don't want to know you.   Ich will nicht wissen, wer du bist.
I don't want to see anyone.   Ich will Niemand sehn!

ORESTES

Hear me out, I have no time. Hear this: Hör mich an, ich hab' nicht Zeit. Hör' zu:

116

(softly)

Orestes lives! [39a]Orestes lebt!

Elektra turns violently. [5]

Don't make a move; they'll guess the Wenn du dich regst, verrätst du ihn.
truth.

ELEKTRA

So he is free! Where is he? So ist er frei? Wo ist er?

ORESTES

He's as free from harm Er ist unversehrt
as I. wie ich.

ELEKTRA

Then rescue him before they've time to So rett' ihn doch, bevor sie ihn erwürgen.
kill him.

ORESTES

By my father's body, that is why I'm [10] Bei meines Vaters Leichnam! Dazu kam
here! ich her!

ELEKTRA
(struck by his tone)

Who are you then? Wer bist denn du?

The old and gloomy servant rushes in silently from the palace, followed by three other servants, prostrates himself before Orestes and kisses his feet. The others kiss his hands and the hem of his garment. Elektra is almost beside herself. [38]

Who are you then? I'm petrified! Wer bist du denn? Ich fürchte mich.

ORESTES
(gently)

The dogs in the yard remember me, Die Hunde auf dem Hof erkennen mich,

(louder)

and my own sister not? [38] udn meine Schwester nicht?

ELEKTRA
(crying out suddenly)

Orest! [33a]Orest!

(very softly, trembling)

Orest! Orest! Orest! Orest! Orest! Orest!
There's no one stirring. Oh, allow my [38] Es rührt sich niemand. O, lass deine
eyes Augen
to see yours! Vision, heaven sends me mich sehn, Traumbild, mir geschenktes
this vision, fairer than all my dreaming! Traumbild, schöner als alle Träume!
Sacred, inexpressible, sublime, majestic Hehres, unbegreifliches, erhabenes
sight! Gesicht,
Oh, stay with me! Do not o bleib' bei mir! Lös' nicht
dissolve in air, don't fade away, don't fade in Luft dich auf, vergeh' mir nicht, vergeh'
away, mir nicht,
for even if this moment death es sei denn, dass ich jetzt gleich
should come and you've revealed yourself sterben muss und du dich anzeigst
and come for me, I die then und mich holen kommst: dann sterbe ich
happier than I have lived! Orest! Orest! Seliger, als ich gelebt! Orest! Orest!
Orest! Orest!

Orestes bends down to Elektra to embrace her. Elektra, vehemently:

No, your arms must not embrace me! [37] Nein, du sollst mich nicht umarmen!
Stand back! I blush for shame before you.[33b]Tritt weg, ich schäme mich vor dir. Ich
I don't weiss nicht,
know how you can look at me. wie du mich ansiehst.
I'm no more than the carcass of your Ich bin nur mehr der Leichnam deiner
sister, Schwester,
my hapless child. I know, mein armes Kind! Ich weiss,

(softly)

you're horrified es schaudert dich
at me, and yet I was a king's own vor mir, und war doch eines Königs
daughter. Tochter.
I think, too, I was fair: when I blew Ich glaube, ich war schön: wenn ich die
out the Lampe

117

night lamp beside my mirror I felt it with	ausblies vor meinem Spiegel, fühlte ich es
an ingenuous wonder. I felt then	mit keuschem Schauer. Ich fühlte es,
how the slender ray of moonlight	wie der dünne Strahl des Mondes
bathed on my body's naked whiteness tenderly,	in meines Körpers weisser Nacktheit badete,
as if upon a millpond. And my hair	so wie in einem Weiher, und mein Haar
was such fine hair, it set the men all trembling,	war solches Haar, vor dem die Männer zittern,
this hair, unkempt, besmirched, degraded.	dies Haar, versträhnt, beschmutzt, erniedrigt.
Do you understand me? I've had to give up	Verstehst du's, Bruder? Ich habe Alles
all I was in dedication. My pure shame	was ich war, hingeben müssen. Meine Scham
I have submitted, the shame that's sweeter	[27a] hab' ich geopfert, die Scham, die süsser
than all things else, the shame which like the silvery haze	als Alles ist, die Scham, die wie der Silberdunst,
that, milky from the moon, encircling every	der milchige des Monds um jedes Weib
woman, keeps away all awful things from her	herum ist und das Grässliche von ihr
and from her spirit. Do you understand me?	und ihrer Seele weghält. Verstehst du's, Bruder?
This sweet sense of wonder I've sacrificed for	[37b] Diese süssen Schauder hab' ich dem Vater
our father. Know then,	opfern müssen. Meinst du,
each time that I rejoiced in my body, all his	wenn ich an meinem Leib mich freute, drangen
sighs forced entry, all of his groanings,	seine Seufzer, drang nicht sein Stöhnen
to my bedside!	an mein Bette?

(sombrely)

For the dead are	Eifersüchtig sind
very jealous, and he sent to me this hate,	[4] die Toten: und er schickte mir den Hass,
this great hollow-eyed hate, as bridegroom.	den hohläugigen Hass als Bräutigam.
So I have now been a prophetess for every hour	So bin ich eine Prophetin immerfort gewesen
since, and from my soul and body I have brought forth	und habe nichts hervorgebracht aus mir
nothing else but curses and despondence.	und meinem Leib als Flüche und Verzweiflung!
What scares you as you look round? Speak to me!	Was schaust du ängstlich um dich? Sprich zu mir!
Tell me! Your body shakes in every limb!	Sprich doch! Du zitterst ja am ganzen Leib?

ORESTES

Just let this body shake. It knows	[39] Lass zittern diesen Leib! Er ahnt,
on which path I must lead it.	welchen Weg ich ihn führe.

ELEKTRA

You'll do it then? Alone? Alone, poor child!	[18] Du wirst es tun? Allein? Du armes Kind?

ORESTES

They who imposed this deed on me, the gods,	Die diese Tat mir auferlegt, die Götter,
will be there with me, to assist me.	werden da sein, mir zu helfen.

ELEKTRA

You'll do it then! He is blessed who does it.	Du wirst es tun! Der ist selig, der tun darf.

ORESTES

It shall be done, it shall be quickly done!	Ich will es tun, ich will es eilig tun.

ELEKTRA

The deed is like a cradle in which the soul reposes,	Die Tat ist wie ein Better, auf dem die Seele ausruht,
like a bed of balsam which the soul can rest upon	wie ein Bett von Balsam, drauf die Seele ruhen kann,
when it's an open wound, a blight, an ulcer or a fire!	die eine Wunde ist, ein Brand, ein Eiter, eine Flamme!

ORESTES

I'll carry it out! I'll carry it out!	Ich werde es tun! Ich werde es tun!

ELEKTRA
(in a frenzy)

He is blessed, he who has come to do it;	[40] Der ist selig, der seine Tat zu tun kommt,
blessed he, who for him yearns;	[10] selig der, der ihn ersehnt,
blessed, who him beholds!	[38] selig, der ihn erschaut!
Blessed, who knows who he is;	Selig, wer ihn erkennt,
blessed, who knows his fine touch!	selig, wer ihn berührt!
Blessed he who may dig from the earth the axe;	Selig, wer ihm das Beil aus der Erde gräbt,
blessed, who for him holds the torch;	selig, wer ihm die Fackel hält,
blessed, blessed who for him opens the door.	selig, selig, wer ihm öffnet die Tür.

The Tutor of Orestes, a strong old man with fiery eyes, stands in the gateway.

TUTOR
(angrily, to them both)

Are you demented, that you don't subdue	[41] Seid ihr von Sinnen, dass ihr euren Mund nicht bändigt, wo ein Hauch, ein Laut, ein Nichts
your voices, where a breath, a sound, or none,	
might wreck our work and us as well.	uns und das Werk verderben kann.

(to Orestes, in headlong haste)

She waits inside there. Her maids are searching for you.	Sie wartet drinnen, ihre Mägde suchen nach dir.
There is no man in there, Orest!	Es ist kein Mann im Haus, Orest!

Orestes draws himself up, conquering his horror. A light shines by the palace door. A servant appears with a torch and the Confidante behind her. Elektra starts back into the shadows. The Confidante bows low to the strangers, making a sign to them to follow. Orestes and the Tutor go inside. The Servant fastens the torch to an iron ring in the doorpost. Orestes closes his eyes for a moment, as though giddy; the Tutor is close behind him. They exchange rapid glances and the door closes behind them. Elektra, alone in horrible excitement, runs to and fro in front of the door with bowed head, like a captive beast in a cage. [1c, 38, 34, 26b, 20, 25]

ELEKTRA
(pausing suddenly)

I couldn't give the axe to him to do it!	Ich habe ihm das Beil nicht geben können!
They have gone in there, and I could not give	Sie sind gegangen und ich habe ihm
the axe to him to do it. There are no	das Beil nicht geben können. Es sind keine
gods in heaven!	Götter in Himmel!

More fearful suspense. From far away inside resounds a shriek from Klytemnestra. Elektra cries aloud like one possessed. [3]

Another blow!	Triff noch einmal!

Elektra stands in the doorway with her back pressed against the door. There is a second cry from within. Chrysothemis and a group of attendants rush out of the building on the left.

CHRYSOTHEMIS

Something must have happened there!	Es muss etwas geschehen sein.

FIRST MAID SERVANT

She cries   Sie schreit
thus in her sleep.   so aus dem Schlaf.

SECOND MAID SERVANT

There must be men inside there.   Es müssen Männer drin sein.
I'm sure I heard some men go in there.   Ich habe Männer gehen hören.

THIRD MAID SERVANT

All   Alle
the doors are barred and bolted.   Türen sind verriegelt.

FOURTH MAID SERVANT

There are murderers,   Es sind Mörder!
there are murderers in there!   Es sind Mörder im Haus!

FIRST MAID SERVANT
(*shrieking*)

Oh!   Oh!

ALL

What's wrong?   Was ist?

FIRST MAID SERVANT

Don't you all see, there in the door,   Seht ihr denn nicht: dort in der Tür steht
one's standing!   einer!

CHRYSOTHEMIS

That is Elektra!   Das ist Elektra!

FIRST, SECOND AND FOURTH MAID SERVANTS

Elektra!   [2c]   Elektra!

CHRYSOTHEMIS

Oh, yes, that's Elektra, Elektra!   Das ist ja Elektra, Elektra!

FIRST, SECOND AND FOURTH MAID SERVANTS

Elektra! But why does she not speak?   Elektra! Warum spricht sie denn nicht?

CHRYSOTHEMIS

Elektra,   Elektra,
but why don't you speak?   warum sprichst du denn nicht?

FOURTH MAID SERVANT

I'll fetch some men,   Ich will hinaus
they'll assist us.   [41] Männer holen!

She runs off to the right.

CHRYSOTHEMIS

Open up the door now,   Mach uns doch die Tür auf,
Elektra!   Elektra!

MAID SERVANTS

Elektra, let us inside!   Elektra, lass uns ins Haus!

CHRYSOTHEMIS

Elektra!   Elektra!

FOURTH MAID SERVANT
(*returning*)

Go back!   Zurück!

Aegisth! Get back inside our quarters, quick!
Aegisth is in the yard.

Aegisth! Zurück in unsre Kammern! Schnell!
Aegisth kommt durch den Hof!

OTHER MAID SERVANTS

Aegisth!

Aegisth!

FOURTH MAID SERVANT

If he should find us,
and if there's something up inside the house,
he'll have us murdered!

Wenn er uns findet
und wenn im Hause was geschehen ist,

lässt er uns töten!

CHRYSOTHEMIS

Go back!

Zurück!

ALL

Go back, go back!

Zurück! Zurück!

They disappear into the building to the left. Aegisthus appears at the gate of the courtyard to the right.

AEGISTHUS
(pausing in the doorway)

Hey, lights there! Lights there!
Is no one there to light me? Doesn't one of these
blackguards move a muscle? Has this race
not learnt discipline yet?

[7] He! Lichter! Lichter!
[41b]Ist Niemand da, zu leuchten? Rührt sich keiner
von allen diesen schuften? Kann das Volk
keine Zucht annehmen?

Elektra takes the torch from the ring and, running towards him, bows low before him. Aegisthus starts back in terror at the sight of the wild figure in the flickering light.

Whoever is that weird woman in here?
I gave an order that forbade an unfamiliar
face ever to come near me!

Was ist das für ein unheimliches Weib?
Ich hab' verboten, dass ein unbekanntes

Gesicht mir in die Nähe kommt!

(recognising her, angrily)

What, you?
Who called on you to come and meet me?

Was, du?
Wer heisst dich, mir entgegentreten?

ELEKTRA

May I not light you?

Darf ich nicht leuchten?

AEGISTHUS

Well, this news concerns you
more than all the others here. Perhaps you
know where the men are who bring news
about Orestes?

Nun, dich geht die Neuigkeit
ja doch vor allen an. Wo find ich
die fremden Männer, die das von Orest
uns melden?

ELEKTRA

Inside. They have found a charming
hostess in there, and they amuse themselves
with her.

Drinnen. Eine liebe Wirtin
[27b]fanden sie vor, und sie ergetzen sich
mit ihr.

AEGISTHUS

And did they say for certain that he
is really dead, and did they say that there's
no doubt of it?

Und melden also wirklich, dass er
gestorben ist, und melden so, dass nicht
zu zweifeln ist?

121

Pauline Tinsley as Elektra with Welsh National Opera in the Netherlands Opera production by Harry Kupfer (photo: Julian Sheppard)

ELEKTRA

Oh, sir, they do not say it just
with words, no, but clear tokens and
gestures
which render thoughts of doubt
impossible.

O Herr, sie melden's nicht
mit Worten bloss, nein, mit leibhaftigen
Zeichen,
an denen auch kein Zweifel möglich ist.

AEGISTHUS

What is that in your voice? And what is
this transformation, that you seem to
emulate
me? What makes you stagger to and fro
here with your light?

Was hast du in der Stimme? Und was ist
in dich gefahren, dass du nach dem Mund
mir redest? Was taumelst du so hin
und her mit deinem Licht?

ELEKTRA

It's really nothing more
than that at last I saw sense, and whose
side
I am on, and whose the strong side is.
Allow me
to light the way before you.

Es ist nichts anderes,
als dass ich endlich klug ward und zu denen
mich halte, die die Stärkeren sind.
Erlaubst du,
[18] dass ich voran dir leuchte?

AEGISTHUS
(slightly hesitating)

To the door.

Bis zur Tür.

Elektra dances an uncanny dance around him and suddenly stoops low.

What dance is that? Watch out there!

Was tanzest du? Gib Obacht.

ELEKTRA

Here's the stairway, mind you don't fall.

Hier! die Stufen dass du nicht fällst.

AEGISTHUS
(at the door)

But why is there no light?
Who are those there?

Warum ist hier kein Licht?
Wer sind die dort?

ELEKTRA

Those in person are they
who'd like to pay respect to you, sir.
And I,
who with insolent impetuousness disturbed
you
often, I at last will learn now, when
the proper moment's come to take my
leave.

Die sind's, die in Person
die aufzuwarten wünschen, Herr. Und
[38] ich,
die so oft durch freche unbescheidne Näh'
dich störte, will nun endlich lernen, mich
im rechten Augenblick zurückzuziehen.

Aegisthus goes in. Silence. Then a noise within. Aegisthus appears at a small window, tearing away the curtain and crying:

AEGISTHUS

Help! Murder! Help your master! Murder, [41]
murder!
They're murdering me! Don't you hear
me?
Don't you hear me?

Helft! Mörder! Helft dem Herren! Mörder,
Mörder!
Sie morden mich! Hört mich niemand?

Hört mich niemand?

He is dragged away.

ELEKTRA
(starting violently)

Agamemnon hears you! [1]

Agamemnon hört dich!

The face of Aegisthus appears once more at the window.

123

AEGISTHUS

Help me!   Weh mir!

Aegisthus is dragged away again. Elektra stands facing the palace, breathing heavily. The women come rushing out of the house to the left, with Chrysothemis among them. As though bereft of their senses they run to the gate of the courtyard. There they suddenly halt and turn.

CHRYSOTHEMIS

Elektra, sister, come with us! Oh, come	Elektra! Schwester! Komm mit uns! O komm
with us! It is our brother in the house!	mit uns! Es ist der Bruder drim im Haus!
It is Orest who has done it!	Es ist Orest, der es getan hat!

Noise in the house. Confused voices, from among which cries of 'Orest! Orest!' occasionally emerge more distinctly. [32a]

Come!	Komm!
He's in the hallway, all are gathered round,	Er stehlt im Vorsaal, alle sind um ihn,
and plant his feet with kisses.	und küssen seine Füsse.

The noise of battle, the combat to the death between the slaves who are faithful to Orestes and the retinue of Aegisthus, has gradually retreated towards the inner courts, with which the door to the right communicates.

All of those	Alle, die
Aegisth had taught to hate him hurled themselves	Aegisth von Herzen hassten, haben sich
like devils on the others. Everywhere,	geworfen auf die andern, überall,
in all the courtyards, there are bodies, [41b]	in allen Höfen liegen Tote, alle,
all those alive have spattered blood on them	die leben, sind mit Blut bespritzt und haben
and are themselves wounded, and yet all are radiant,	selbst Wunden, und doch strahlen alle, alle
all are embracing and rejoicing. A thousand torches	umarmen sich und jauchzen. Tausend Fackeln
are brightly burning. Don't you hear?	sind angezündet. Hörst du nicht? So hörst
So don't you then hear?	du denn nicht?

The noise outside increases, but when Elektra begins it retreats more and more to the outer courts to the right and in the background. The other women have run out, leaving Chrysothemis alone. The light comes from outside.

ELEKTRA
(crouching on the threshold)

Do I not hear it? How could I	Ob ich nicht höre? Ob ich die
not hear the music? It's coming from me.	Musik nicht höre? Sie kommt doch aus mir.
The thousands who are bearing torches [38]	Die Tausende, die Fackeln tragen
on high, whose footsteps, whose innumerable	und deren Tritte, deren uferlose
untold myriad footsteps make the earth [11]	Myriaden Tritte überall die Erde
resound with such hollow rumbling, all [10]	dumpf dröhnen machen, alle warten
are waiting	
for me. I know it, that they all are waiting,	auf mich: ich weiss doch, dass sie alle warten,
for I must lead the dancing, and I	Weil ich den Reigen führen muss, und ich
cannot. The ocean, the mighty [27]	kann nicht, der Ozean, der ungeheure,
infinite twentyfold ocean, has buried	der zwanzigfache Ozean begröbt
all my limbs with its great weight. I cannot	mir jedes Glied mit seiner Wucht, ich kann mich
uplift them! [41b]	nicht heben!

CHRYSOTHEMIS
(almost shrieking with excitement)

Can you not hear? They are holding him, [21]	Hörst du denn nicht? Sie tragen ihn,
they're holding him on high above them!	sie tragen ihn auf ihren Händen.

124

ELEKTRA

(leaping up, to herself, without heeding Chrysothemis)

We are with the gods, we accomplishers. Wir sind bei den Göttern, wir Vollbringenden.

(enthusiastically)

They drive themselves deep into us like [39b]Sie fahren dahin wie die Schärfe des Schwerts
a sword's sharp blade, the gods, but their durch uns, die Götter, aber ihre
fine magnificence is not too much for us! Herrlichkeit ist nicht zuviel für uns!

CHRYSOTHEMIS

Every face is completely transfigured. Every Allen sind die Gesichter verwandelt, allen
eyelid is glistening, and the oldest cheeks schimmern die Augen und die alten Wangen
run with teardrops! All are crying. Don't you hear? vor Tränen! Alle weinen, hörst du's nicht?

ELEKTRA

I've sown the seeds of darkest gloom Ich habe Finsternis gesät
and reap a harvest of joy! und ernte Lust über Lust!

CHRYSOTHEMIS

Good are the gods, good! Gut sind die Götter! Gut!

ELEKTRA

I was a black cadaver in the living, Ich war ein schwarzer Leichnam unter Lebenden
but this very moment I am the fire of life und diese Stunde bin ich das Feuer des Lebens
and my bright flame is consuming the darkness und meine Flamme verbrennt die Finsternis
of the world. My complexion's whiter far der Welt. Mein Gesicht muss weisser sein
than the shining pale moon's white face. als das weissglühende Gesicht des Monds.

CHRYSOTHEMIS

A new life starts now for you and Es fängt ein Leben für dich und
me, and all the people here. mich und alle Menschen an.
The mighty, ever-bounteous gods it is [10] Die überschwänglich guten Götter sinds,
to whom we are indebted. die das gegeben haben.
Whoever cared for us? Wer hat uns je geliebt?

ELEKTRA

If someone should see me, he must prepare Wenn einer auf mich sieht, muss er den Tod
to greet death or he must pass out from joy. empfangen oder muss vergehen vor Lust.

CHRYSOTHEMIS

Whoever cared for us? Wer hat uns je geliebt?

ELEKTRA

Do you see then my face? Seht ihr denn mein Gesicht?
Look at the light which pours out from me! Seht ihr das Licht, das von mir ausgeht?

CHRYSOTHEMIS

Now our dear brother's here, and love Nun ist der Bruder da, und Liebe
flows over us both like oil and balsam. Love fliesst über uns wie Öl und Myrrhen. Liebe
is the answer! What is living without loving? ist Alles! Wer kann leben ohne Liebe?

ELEKTRA
(wildly)

Ai! Love is fatal! And yet no one dies without
first making love's acquaintanceship.

Ai! Liebe tötet! Aber keiner fährt dahin
und hat die Liebe nicht gekannt!

CHRYSOTHEMIS

Elektra, I must go to my brother now.

[38] Elektra! Ich muss bei meinem Bruder stehn!

Chrysothemis runs off. Elektra descends from the threshold, throwing back her head like a Maenad, thrusting her knees high in forward movement, flinging her arms wide apart: it is a dance of indescribably intensity. Chrysothemis appears again at the door. Behind her torches, crowds of men and women.

CHRYSOTHEMIS

Elektra!

Elektra!

ELEKTRA
(She ceases her dance and stares at her.)

Silence, and dance now! Everyone must come here! Here, close to me! I carry the load
of fortune, and I dance before you here. With happiness like ours, just one thing seems right:
silence and dancing...

[11] Schweig, und tanze. Alle müssen
[12] herbei! Hier schliesst euch an! Ich trage die Last
des Glückes, und ich tanze vor euch her. Wer glücklich ist wie wir, dem ziemt nur eins:
schweigen und tanzen ...

Elektra dances a few more steps of supreme triumph and falls lifeless. Chrysothemis rushes to her side then hurries to the door of the palace and batters on it. [39b, 11, 4, 9, 24b]

CHRYSOTHEMIS

Orest! Orest!

[1a] Orest! Orest!

Silence. Curtain.

The House of Atreus in the production by Günther Rennert, designed by Rudolf Heinrich at the Bayerische Staatsoper, Munich, 1972 (photo: Sabine Toepffer)

Strauss's Orchestra
in 'Salome' and 'Elektra'

Jonathan Burton

Richard Strauss must be unique in operatic history: he began his mature operatic career when he was already established as an unrivalled composer of orchestral music. Indeed, outside the opera house his fame still rests on the great tone poems — *Don Juan, Death and Transfiguration, Till Eulenspiegel, Also sprach Zarathustra, Don Quixote* and *Ein Heldenleben*. This succession of masterpieces had given him a sure hand in the deployment of the late-Romantic orchestra; the narrative elements of *Till Eulenspiegel* and *Don Quixote* had enabled him to develop an unsurpassed facility in the use of instrumental effects for detailed 'programmatic' tone-painting.

In 1904 — while he was working on *Salome* — Strauss prepared a new German edition of Berlioz's *Traité d'instrumentation* of 1842. Ostensibly, Strauss's modest aim was to bring Berlioz's pioneering work up to date, but the result makes fascinating reading; again and again, Berlioz's understanding of the capabilities and foibles of each instrument stimulates Strauss to add comments from his own experience. The work also reveals his tastes; he quotes examples not only from the scores of Berlioz himself but from those of composers as diverse as Bizet, Marschner, Verdi and Liszt (whose orchestration he praises to the detriment of Brahms and Schumann) — and above all Wagner, who inspires in him a remarkable degree of adulation:

> Richard Wagner's scores are the alpha and omega of my additions to this work; they embody the only important progress in the art of instrumentation since Berlioz.

From this extraordinary edition we gain a wealth of technical information unavailable elsewhere, and a valuable insight into Strauss's own methods. His debt to Wagner is also evident in the orchestral texture of his early opera, *Guntram*; but by 1904 he had evolved the distinctive, brilliant and colourful orchestral technique which would enable him to compose *Salome* and *Elektra* as 'Stage Tone Poems' (in Norman Del Mar's phrase), by adding the element of sung drama to the pictorial and lyrical use of the orchestra he had developed in his orchestral works.

Strauss's 'pictorialism' comes so naturally to him that a single word is often enough to spark off an orchestral image: any mention of dogs in either *Salome* or *Elektra*, for instance, will set up an appropriate barking somewhere in the orchestra — whether the rather feeble solo bassoon early in *Elektra*, the *piano* trombone chord for Orestes' 'hounds at the gate', or the full-throated baying of six muted horns as Salome threatens to throw the head of Jokanaan to the 'watchdogs'. Similarly, as Salome likens Jokanaan's hair to the cedars of Lebanon which give shade to lions, we hear the snarl of the lions in the brass — *pp* crescendo to *sforzando*. Such animal noises came easily to the composer who had portrayed an entire flock of sheep in *Don Quixote*; other echoes of *Quixote* can be detected in the 'icy wind' Herod thinks he feels, or the storm shaking the hut which Chrysothemis imagines, recalling Don Quixote's ride through the air on a magic horse; or the adventure of Quixote and Sancho Panza in a leaky boat, whose watery music is incongruously recalled (low divided strings and woodwind) as Jokanaan speaks of Jesus 'in a vessel on the sea of Galilæa'. But besides these naturalistic effects — and such obvious pictorialism as the clinking of Klytemnestra's talismans (harps, glockenspiel, pizzicato strings and a fluttering flute) — Strauss also uses the orchestra to build up a powerful sense of atmosphere, a skill he had first exercised in the tone poems *Death and Transfiguration* and *Zarathustra*. Virtually the whole of *Salome* is given an unearthly, brooding quality by sheer orchestral colour, but the most striking *tour de force* is the narration of Klytemnestra's dream in *Elektra*: for some hundred bars, an atmosphere of evil, unease and oppressiveness is engendered by muted strings, low muted brass and predominantly dark woodwind colours (without recourse to the conventional orchestrator's 'spooky' props such as wind machine, tam-tam or cymbal roll).

* * *

'Conduct *Salome* and *Elektra* as if they were by Mendelssohn: fairy music.' Strauss's advice (in his *Ten Golden Rules for the Album of a Young Conductor*) may seem odd in view of the huge size of the orchestra (ideally 105 players for *Salome*, 111 for *Elektra*, though these numbers would be a tight fit in any orchestra pit and are impossibly large for most). Strauss does not use his massive forces merely as noise-makers: he is seeking to extend the range of possibilities available to him in each section, to achieve the 'coruscating lightness and delicacy' praised by William Mann as well as extremes of pitch, dynamics and tone-colour. In his edition of the Berlioz *Treatise*, Strauss stresses the value of economy in the use of orchestral effects, approving Wagner's 'wise application of the triangle' in restricting its appearance in Act Two of *Siegfried* to a single note at the end. Nevertheless, the sheer bulk of Strauss's orchestra presents unavoidable problems of balance with the singers, as he was to recognise in operas such as *Ariadne auf Naxos* and *Intermezzo*, where he deliberately cut down the orchestral sound to 'chamber-music' textures. Although he insisted that in *Salome* and *Elektra*, with correct observance of his dynamic markings, the words would still be heard, later in life he conceded that 'forty percent audibility' was a realistic target. He wryly told against himself the story of the dress rehearsal of *Elektra*, at which the conductor Ernst von Schuch acceded to Strauss's requests for 'more orchestral detail' with such alacrity that even the composer had to admit that the singers were being drowned: '"You see", said Schuch triumphantly, and the first performance had perfect balance.'

Strauss would certainly have agreed with Rimsky-Korsakov's emphatic statement in the preface to his *Principles of Orchestration*: 'In the orchestra there is no such thing as ugly quality of tone.' Despite his striving for 'expressionistic' effects, Strauss was a late-Romantic orchestrator, never forgetting that the orchestra had evolved as a corporate instrument for making beautiful sounds; notwithstanding occasional markings such as 'hässlich kreischend' ('screeching hideously'), for woodwind imitating the voice of Herodias, he never required his players to make unmusical or ugly sounds. He was then at the forefront of advances in orchestral technique: besides adopting Wagner's achievements in the development of new instruments, he was quick to spot new inventions that suited his purpose, such as the heckelphone. Even such now-familiar instruments as the xylophone, celeste and pedal timpani were relative newcomers, while the basset-horn — a low-pitched clarinet —

Josephine Barstow as Salome with Emile Belcourt as Herod at ENO (photo: John Garner)

had been languishing in virtual oblivion since Mozart's use of it over a century earlier.

* * *

Although the orchestras in *Salome* and *Elektra* are the largest Strauss ever called for in the theatre, it is interesting to note the differences between the two scores. *Salome* is glittering, kaleidoscopic, oriental, and progresses in flashes of light, whereas *Elektra* is dark and monumental, moving in larger slabs of homogeneous orchestral colour. The orchestra of *Elektra* is more of a heavy blunt instrument than that of *Salome*; Wagnerian power is assured by a quartet of Wagner tubas, a bass trumpet and a contrabass trombone, while the flexibility and carrying power of the woodwind is augmented by the addition of two basset-horns to the (already enlarged) clarinet section. *Elektra* also has a darker colouring overall because of the unusual disposition of its string resources.

The **strings** have formed the backbone of all orchestras since the 17th century; in Strauss's hands, the string orchestra becomes an immensely flexible, eloquent body of sound, capable of infinite gradations of expression — from the onomatopoeic 'scharrend' ('scratching') as Elektra digs for the buried axe, the queasy chromatic *tremolandi* for the blood of Agamemnon, or the tapping *col legno* (with the back of the bow) to convey Herod's horror at the idea of a severed head, to the gentle chamber-music texture of divided soloists at Elektra's words to Chrysothemis, 'I'll be a proper sister from now on' ('Von jetzt an will ich deine Schwester sein'). (Strauss's direction reads 'All strings very heartfelt, with a lot of *vibrato* — don't use open strings!') In fact, so rich is the sound of the carpet of divided strings that the simple string orchestra becomes a refreshing contrast in itself — most movingly as Chrysothemis longs for a life of freedom outside the confines of the Palace of Atreus, 'I have a fire within my breast' ('Ich hab's wie Feuer in der Brust').

For *Salome*, Strauss specifies the number of string players as 16 first violins, 16 second violins, 10 or 12 violas, 10 celli and 8 basses; this would be fairly normal (if large) on a concert platform. The score of *Elektra*, however, breaks from normality with an unusual specification: 24 violins (divided into three groups instead of two), 18 violas (also divided in three), 12 celli (divided in two) and 8 basses. Compared to the *Salome* line-up, this gives more weight to the middle and lower registers, thus partly accounting for *Elektra*'s overall darker colouring. But Strauss has an extraordinary trick up his sleeve: he directs that the first group of six violas should also play violins, becoming a fourth group of violins, and changing the distribution to a more nearly 'normal' 30 violins plus 12 violas — almost as in *Salome*. Strauss uses this change only twice: at the recognition scene between Orestes and Elektra, and in Elektra's triumphant dance. Thus for these two scenes he lifts the entire orchestral texture to a lighter, sunnier plane. (Even assuming, however, that there is enough room in the pit for all these players and their instrument cases, not all viola players are equally proficient on the violin — and the 'fourth violin' part goes too high to be played on the viola; the inevitable compromise solutions must diminish the impact of Strauss's finely-calculated special effect.)

The sound of massed violins in expansive lyrical flight is the staple voice of the Straussian orchestra, and he uses it to the full — often carrying them to stratospheric heights, as in the apotheoses of both heroines. He also uses

Neil Howlett as Jokanaan at ENO in the production by Joachim Herz, designed by Rudolf Heinrich, 1981 (photo: Donald Southern)

groups of solo violins to great effect (four solo violins, magically combined with muted trumpets, for Salome's 'Geheimnis der Liebe' — the 'secret of love'). A *single* solo violin is reserved for special moments of tenderness or 'personal' characterisation (as it had been in *Zarathustra* and *Ein Heldenleben*) — when Elektra embraces her sister's slim hips, or representing the voice of Jesus when Jokanaan describes Him preaching to His disciples.

One very odd habit of the composer can be observed in *Salome*: writing non-existent notes for the violins. The E in this example is a third below the lowest open string:

In fact the tune is doubled elsewhere in the orchestra, and, as Norman Del Mar explains, Strauss did not actually expect the violins to include the unplayable note:

> In his more patient moments he would explain that if the player *thought* the unobtainable note strongly enough and tried hard to look as if he *was* playing it, the audience would never know it was missing.
>
> *Anatomy of the Orchestra*, 1981

131

Hildegard Behrens as Salome with Walter Raffeiner as Herod and Brigitte Fassbaender as Herodias at the Bayerische Staatsoper, Munich in 1987 (photo: Sabine Toepffer)

Conversely, in a similar passage in *Elektra*, Strauss evidently did intend the bottom note to be played —

— since he instructs the players to tune the G string down to the low F.

Mellower and less powerful than the violins, the violas have less chance to be heard in Strauss's scores but their rich *divisi* contributes to the dark colouring of *Elektra*, and provides a warm chordal support for Jokanaan's prophecies in *Salome*. The fragile sound of a solo viola can be heard as Salome looks at the moon, and later as an extraordinarily sinister *ostinato* as she begins her dance:

A solo viola is joined by a solo cello to convey a tender intimacy in Elektra's reunion with Orestes; the celli in their upper register have a magnificent singing 'tenor' quality unrivalled in the other strings. Conversely, divided celli moving in their lower register provide the rippling background for Jokanaan's

132

utterances; and at the very end of the opera, for the brooding *pianissimo* chords just before Salome's final outburst, Strauss divides his low muted celli into as many as nine separate parts — a dense, ghostly sound.

Whilst Elektra is waiting for Orestes to complete the killing of Klytemnestra and Aegisthus, her impatient pacing ('like a captive beast in a cage') is depicted by a scurrying of celli and double-basses in their lowest register. The double-basses naturally spend most of their time, self-effacingly, as the sheet-anchor

Michael Devlin as Jokanaan with Gwyneth Jones as Salome, San Francisco, 1987 (photo: David Powers)

of the harmony at the bottom of the orchestra, but Strauss does manage to give them the occasional moment of glory. It is for the double-bass that he reserves his most controversial special effect — which, it is amusing if not altogether surprising to discover, he had stolen unashamedly from Berlioz. In the *Treatise*, Berlioz had reported:

> A Piedmontese artist, M. Langlois, who played in Paris about fifteen years ago, produced very peculiar high tones of incredible power on the double-bass (with the bow) by pinching the highest string between the thumb and forefinger of the left hand . . . If there were need to render in the orchestra the violent outcry of a female voice, no other instrument could produce it better than the double-bass treated in this fashion.

Strauss specifies exactly this effect as Salome waits expectantly for the head of Jokanaan; first one solo bass, then successively three more, produce a 'pinched' high B♭ —

— 'with a short sharp stroke of the bow, so that a sound is produced which resembles a woman's suppressed moans and cries'. It is a most peculiar sound.

* * *

The **woodwind** section of the Classical orchestra consisted of pairs of flutes, oboes, clarinets and bassoons. In his tone poems, Strauss had already augmented this to quadruple forces, including other members of each woodwind family: the piccolo above the flutes (though, oddly enough, not the alto flute below them), the cor anglais below the oboes, both the high E♭ clarinet and the bass clarinet, and the contrabassoon taking the 'double-bass' role below the bassoons.

The flutes are the obvious choice for any reference to 'birds', particularly in *Salome*, in sinister flutter-tongued arpeggios as Jokanaan prophesies that the 'brood of the Basilisk shall then devour the birds of the forest':

— and there is an almost conventional extended flute solo during Salome's Dance (where it does not have to compete with a soprano voice). Herod's call for 'torches' is answered by an octave leap of three flutes in a triad, conveying the momentary blaze with telling economy. The piccolo fulfils its natural function of sparkle at the top of woodwind chording, as well as briefly making a hollow-voiced solo appearance for Salome's 'I am not hungry, Tetrarch'.

The oboe family, in both operas, is further augmented by the addition of a heckelphone below the cor anglais. This magnificent instrument — a bass oboe, four feet long — was invented by the bassoon-maker Wilhelm Heckel, apparently at Wagner's suggestion, and had been perfected only a year before its first appearance in *Salome* in 1905. It makes a memorable impression at, 'I am not thirsty, Tetrarch':

Elsewhere it is a sonorous bass to the oboe section, and its dark hollow tone casts an unearthly light over the proceedings. The oboe family, playing as a section, is much in evidence in *Salome*, from their noble announcement of Jokanaan's leitmotif as he is brought out of the cistern, to their spiky accompaniment to the disputation of the Jews. In *Elektra*, by contrast, a plaintive solo oboe touchingly conveys the despair of Chrysothemis as she bewails their trapped existence 'like captive birds'.

The clarinet family gains the greatest number of extra instruments in these scores; the usual pair is doubled and Strauss adds a high clarinet in E♭ (its solos always reminiscent of its twin, the D clarinet, in *Till Eulenspiegel*), a bass clarinet (heard meandering gloomily in the depths as Salome looks down into the cistern), and — for *Elektra* — two basset-horns, to bring the number of clarinets in the pit to an astonishing total of eight. A solo clarinet is the first sound to be heard in *Salome*:

— and its eerie chill tone pervades the score, announcing themes, leaping up and down accompanying figurations with unrivalled agility, or merely holding a trill of sinister anticipation when 'something terrible' is about to happen. Used as a group, the massed clarinet choir has a distinctive flavour, spooky in its lowest register for a chordal theme associated with Klytemnestra, or conveying a vivid sense of exaggerated courtliness when Herod invites Salome to drink wine with him. (There is an extravagantly complicated bass clarinet part here, with a footnote that if the player is not 'quite excellent' the entire passage may be omitted.)

The bassoons are rather overshadowed by all this opulence above them; apart from the querulous 'dog' in the first scene of *Elektra*, and a similar portrayal of 'stammering', their solo voice is rarely heard. Below them, however, the contrabassoon has a magnificent part — going right down to the lowest A, the same as the bottom note of a piano and the deepest note obtainable on any orchestral instrument. It takes the spotlight for two striking solos in *Salome*, both associated with Jokanaan's cistern. The first solo carries a footnote suggesting that if the player is 'not outstanding' the part should be given to the first bassoon; perhaps, like the bass clarinet passage mentioned above, this is a deliberate piece of 'orchestral psychology' to spur the player to excellence (there is a similar footnote to a contrabassoon solo in *Elektra*).

* * *

'Never look encouragingly at the **brass**', exhorts Strauss in another of his *Ten Golden Rules*, well aware that they constitute the most powerful orchestral section (and the one most likely to drown the singers). He writes for a massive brass section in *Salome* (six horns, four trumpets, four trombones and tuba), which is augmented for *Elektra* to eight horns, four Wagner tubas (played by four of the horn players), six trumpets plus a bass trumpet (three of the trumpets being reserved for the closing pages), three trombones plus a contrabass trombone, and a contrabass tuba; but he cleverly restrains their volume in accompanying passages, saving their moments of greatest glory for interludes in which singers do not have to compete.

Strauss's father had played principal horn for Wagner (whom he detested), and had instilled in his son a lifetime's working knowledge of the instrument. For Jokanaan's utterances in *Salome*, and for the 'monumental' music of the early scenes in *Elektra*, Strauss deliberately cultivates a Wagnerian chordal horn texture — solid, rich and warm. Elsewhere, he fully exploits their capabilities: the barking of hounds in both operas, whoops and trills of joy as Salome gets her wish and Herod despatches the executioner to Jokanaan, a lyrical solo horn for the first statement of Elektra's 'dance' theme, and everywhere the Straussian fanfare-motifs familiar from *Don Juan* and *Ein Heldenleben*.

The quartet of Wagner tubas in *Elektra* is a rarity: Strauss was to use them again only in *Die Frau ohne Schatten* and the *Alpine Symphony*. These unwieldy but noble instruments were invented by Wagner to add weight to the horns in the *Ring*; Strauss noted that their tone could be 'hoarse and rancorous' as well as 'solemn and majestic', employing these contrasting colours in association with, respectively, Klytemnestra and Orestes. Unusually, he also prescribes mutes for them — a peculiar ghostly noise, appropriate to Klytemnestra's 'dream narration'.

Strauss's handling of the trumpets is almost as resourceful as that of the horns. They come into their own for evocations of royal power or nobility; but Strauss was equally aware of the ability of a solo trumpet to soar over the full orchestra with a lyrical melody, as at Salome's moment of triumph before she kisses the mouth of Jokanaan, or just before Elektra recognises Orestes. He also gives the trumpets their share of onomatopoeic effects, such as a fleeting muted chord at Elektra's 'wie ein Schatten' ('like a shadow'), or when Orestes is described as having been 'dragged by his horses' —

— 'schleifen' ('dragging') signifying a *portamento*.

Leonie Rysanek as Salome and Dietrich Fischer-Dieskau as Jokanaan at the Bayerische Staatsoper, Munich in the production by Günther Rennert, designed by Rudolf Heinrich (photo: Anne Kirchbach)

The bass trumpet was also invented by Wagner for the *Ring*; Strauss had experimented with it in *Macbeth* (an early tone poem) and *Guntram*, and uses its imperious tones in *Elektra* to announce Orestes:

He takes care to restrain his trombones and tuba, though when unleashed they have great power, as in the rising 'Agamemnon' theme starting with a juicy low E from contrabass trombone and tuba:

He was also fascinated by the effect of trombone mutes, which he described in 1904 as a recent invention: 'In *forte* they give the trombones a rattling sound, in *pp* a tremendously gruesome, fantastic and gloomy one.' Strauss uses the muted trombones to portray Salome's revulsion of Jokanaan — 'Your hair is hideous,' to stabbing *sforzandi*.

* * *

The remaining instruments — **harps**, **celeste**, **timpani** and **percussion** — might seem to come under the heading of special effects but Strauss (in his annotations to Berlioz) warns orchestrators to:

> use all particularly bright and characteristic colours of the orchestra very sparingly . . . Nowadays all these special orchestral titbits (. . .) are being terribly misused. Especially the percussion instruments should be used only as isolated highlights if their effect is to be felicitous . . . Otherwise the ear of the listener becomes unnecessarily dulled: fine light-accents become formless smears of colour.

Salome does indeed utilise many 'colouristic' instruments to precisely calculated effect. The little splash of celeste and harps which accompanies

138

every reference to 'dance' prepares us unconsciously for the Dionysiac release of energy when Salome finally does dance; Elektra's dance, by contrast, is a much more serious affair, though she, too, gets her harps and celeste — and later a triangle and a tambourine.

Strauss uses two harps — partly for harmonic flexibility, and partly for volume and density of texture; the sound of two harps chasing each other in *glissandi* as Salome cajoles Narraboth is particularly striking, as is their spiky depiction of the 'crown of thorns' of Jokanaan's hair. In Elektra's dance, he even asks that the harps should be 'further doubled if possible' — though few orchestra pits can have room for more than two.

The silvery-toned celeste is another instrument described by Strauss as a recent invention (Tchaikovsky's 'Sugar Plum Fairy' pre-dating *Salome* by only 13 years); Strauss uses it as an adjunct to the harps and for for such miniature tone-pictures as a 'coral branch' and, of course, the 'silver charger' in *Salome*. It appears in *Elektra* only when the first violas have made their switch to fourth violins — adding a glitter to the overall lightening of the texture. For *Salome*, Strauss fleetingly adds two more keyboard instruments: a harmonium at the beginning, offstage (curiously instructed to be 'at the side from which Salome will appear', as if its sound were a ghostly pre-figuring of her actual presence), and, at the very end, an organ, whose deepest pedal tones suffuse Salome's 'geheimnisvolle Musik' with a mysterious aura no other instrument could have produced.

Strauss's treatment of the timpani is a further instance of his inventiveness: he takes the kettledrums far beyond their original role as punctuation, giving them complicated parts (and two separate players to cope with them in *Elektra* — for example at the mention of 'horses', in a galloping figure which eventually develops into a Valkyrian 'ride'). The frequent changes of tuning imply that Strauss requires the recently invented pedal tuning mechanism rather than laborious re-tuning by hand. This facility enables him to give the timpani important melodic figures — as Janáček was to do in *Katya Kabanova* (1919) and on one occasion he has to draw a map of the layout of the drums to show how a figure can be made playable:

The other percussion instruments really do have to be classified as special effects — such as the switch of birch twigs for 'swatting flies' in *Elektra* — and his use of them is always economical. Salome's Dance comes closest to a conventional 'colouristic' use of a large percussion section, with triangle, tambourine, castanets, an extra high timp, and a xylophone — curiously referred to as a 'Holz- und Strohinstrument' ('instrument of wood and straw'): even a generation after Saint-Saëns' *Danse macabre* (1875), the xylophone had not yet assumed the keyboard shape we know today, being simply a collection of tuned wooden bars laid out on a bed of straw. Strauss's ferocious rising

139

scales show considerable faith in the player's dexterity on this primitive instrument:

One final orchestral effect may conclude this survey: the large gong, or tam-tam, makes a terrifying sound when struck normally, but to depict Herod's madness ('It is not cold, it is hot') Strauss directs it to be rubbed with a triangle beater, which produces a ferocious metallic roar. He had tried this out in *Macbeth*; for once it seems to have been his own idea — borrowed from neither Wagner nor Berlioz.

* * *

These scores are the twin peaks of Strauss's achievement as an orchestrator: never again would he use such vast forces as in *Elektra*, or weave such a glittering multicoloured fabric as *Salome*. His experience in writing purely orchestral works, tempered by his parallel career as an operatic conductor, had taught him how to use the orchestra as an immensely flexible instrument, capable of hitherto undreamt-of virtuosity, illuminating countless details with flashes of 'tone-painting' — without drowning his singers in its sheer mass of sound.

Treatise on Instrumentation by Hector Berlioz, enlarged and revised by Richard Strauss; trans. Theodore Font, Kalmus, New York, 1948.

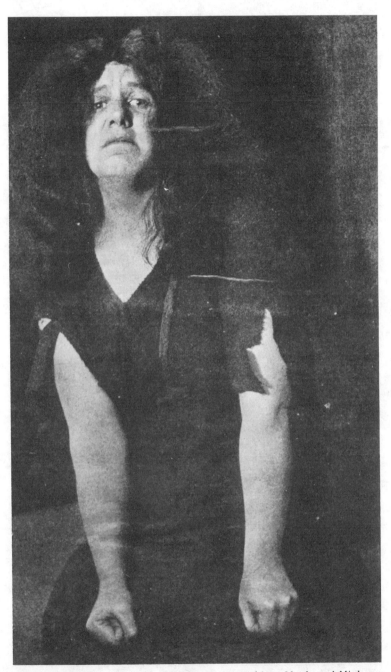

Edyth Walker as Elektra in the London première of 1910 (photo: Mander and Mitchenson Theatre Collection)

Selective Discography

Robert Seeley

'Salome'

Conductor	*G. Solti*	*H. von Karajan*
Orchestra/ Opera House	**Vienna PO**	**Vienna PO**
Date	*1962*	*1978*
Salome	B. Nilsson	H. Behrens
Herod	G. Stolze	K.W. Boehm
Herodias	G. Hoffman	A. Baltsa
Jokanaan	B. Waechter	J. van Dam
Narraboth	W. Kmentt	W. Ochman
Page	J. Veasey	H. Angervo
UK LP Number	Decca SET 228 (2)	EMI SLS 5139 (2)
UK Tape Number	—	EMI TC-SLS 5139 (2)
UK CD Number	Decca 414 414-2 (2)	EMI CDS 749358-2 (2)
US LP Number	—	Angel SBLX 3848 (2)
US Tape Number	—	Angel 4X2X-3848 (2)
US CD Number	London 414 414-2 (2)	—

'Elektra'

Conductor	*G. Solti*	*C. Perick*
Orchestra/ Opera House	**Vienna PO**	**French National**
Date	*1967*	*1984*
Klytemnestra	R. Resnik	M. Forrester
Elektra	B. Nilsson	U. Vinzing
Chrysothemis	M. Collier	L. Rysanek
Aegisthus	G. Stolze	H. Hiestermann
Orestes	T. Krause	B. Norup
UK LP Number	Decca SET 354 (2)	Rodolphe RP 12420/1 (2)
UK Tape Number	—	Rodolphe RPK 12420/1 (2)
UK CD Number	Decca 417 345-2 (2)	Rodolphe RPC 32420/1 (2)
US LP Number	London OSA 1269 (2)	—
US Tape Number	London OSA 5-1269 (2)	—
US CD Number	London 417 345-2 (2)	—

Bibliography

David Nice

Both Norman Del Mar in *Richard Strauss: a critical commentary on his life and works* Volume One (London, 1962, 1978, 1986) and William Mann in *Richard Strauss: a critical study of the operas* (London, 1964), offer detailed studies of the operas and clear summaries of the literary sources; for a briefer introduction to the background and a personal appreciation of the scores, Michael Kennedy's book on Strauss in the *Master Musicians* series (London, 1976) is highly recommended. Strauss himself gives a terse insight into the circumstances of the premières in *Recollections and Reflections* (London, 1953). Sensation and censorship surrounding the first Covent Garden performances are wittily recounted in the elegant, barbed anecdotes of Sir Thomas Beecham, the conductor on those occasions, in his autobiography *A Mingled Chime* (London, 1944, 1987). Production design is well served in the lavishly illustrated *Richard Strauss: the staging of his operas* (London, 1980) by Rudolf Hartmann.

Though the Hofmannsthal-Strauss correspondence is less extensive over *Elektra* than in the collaborations that followed, it still contains many illuminating details and remains available in the translation of Hanns Hammelmann and Ewald Osers, with an introduction by Edward Sackville-West (London, 1961; Cambridge, 1980). Strauss's consultation of his friend Romain Rolland over a French translation for the Paris première of *Salome*, and Rolland's doubts, covert or explicit, over the composer's preoccupation with decadent literature in the two works appear in *Richard Strauss and Romain Rolland: correspondence, diary and essays* edited and annotated by Rollo Myers (London, 1968). The fruitless championship of *Salome* in Vienna by Gustav Mahler, the correspondence between the two conductor-composers and a thorough essay on the relationship by Hertha Blaukopf are to be found in *Mahler-Strauss: correspondence* (London, 1984). Mahler's opinions on Strauss and *Salome* in letters and through the sometimes questionable medium of his wife Alma can be further consulted in Alma Mahler, *Gustav Mahler: memories and letters*, edited by Donald Mitchell (London, 1973).

Oscar Wilde's *Salomé* appears in a Penguin volume of selected Wilde plays (London, 1954); his fascination with the subject has been explored in a recent biography by Richard Ellmann (London, 1987). The original Hofmannsthal play *Elektra* is unavailable in translation, though the three Greek dramatists' handling of the myth can all be found in Penguin paperbacks.

Contributors

Paul Banks is a Lecturer at Goldsmith's College, University of London, and a specialist in the music of Mahler and his contemporaries.

Kenneth Segar is a Lecturer in German at the University of Oxford and a Fellow of St Edmund Hall.

Christopher Wintle is Senior Lecturer in Music at Goldsmith's College, University of London, and a member of the editorial board of *Music Analysis.*

Jonathan Burton is a part-time lecturer at Goldsmith's College, University of London, and the Music Librarian for English National Opera.

Tom Hammond was a member of English National Opera and, as it then was, Sadler's Wells for many years as coach and Music Consultant with a special knowledge of the Rossini repertory. His translations include *Il trovatore, Fidelio* and *Mary Stuart.*

Anthony Hose, conductor, is the Artistic Director of the Buxton Festival and the Beaumaris Festival, Anglesey. His most recent translations for Buxton are Handel's *Ariodante* and Conti's *Don Quixote in Sierra Morena*.

The Richard-Strauss-Institut in Munich, founded in 1983, is an international centre for the study and cultivation of the works of Richard Strauss. It aims at collecting, analysing and evaluating all existing documents and making them available to the public. Visitors who would like to use the extensive library for research purposes are advised to make an appointment. The library is open Mondays to Fridays 1pm to 4pm. Richard Strauss Institut, Sonnenstrasse 10, 8000 München 2. Tel: 089 233 8024 (Administration), 089 233 8987 (Library).